PUBLISHED BY BOOM BOOKS

www.boombooks.biz

ABOUT THE SERIES

.... But after that, I realised that I knew very little about these parents of mine. They had been born about the start of the Twentieth Century, and they died in 1970 and 1980. For their last 50 years, I was old enough to speak with a bit of sense.

I could have talked to them a lot about their lives. I could have found out about the times they lived in. But I did not. I know almost nothing about them really. Their courtship? Working in the pits? The Lock-out in the Depression? Losing their second child? Being dusted as a miner? The shootings at Rothbury? My uncles killed in the War? Love on the dole? There were hundreds, thousands of questions that I would now like to ask them. But, alas, I can't. It's too late.

Thus, prompted by my guilt, I resolved to write these books. They describe happenings that affected people, real people. The whole series is, to coin a modern phrase, designed to push your buttons, to make you remember and wonder at things forgotten. The books might just let nostalgia see the light of day, so that oldies and youngies will talk about the past and re-discover a heritage otherwise forgotten. Hopefully, they will spark discussions between generations, and foster the asking and answering of questions that should not remain unanswered.

BORN IN 1975?

WHAT ELSE HAPPENED?

RON WILLIAMS

AUSTRALIAN SOCIAL HISTORY

BOOK 37 IN A SERIES OF 37

FROM 1939 to 1975

War Babies Years (1939 to 1945):	**7 Titles**
Baby Boom Years (1946 to 1960):	**15 Titles**
Post Boom Years (1961 to 1975):	**15 Titles**

BOOM, BOOM BABY, BOOM

Published by Boom Books.
Wickham, NSW, Australia

Web: www.boombooks.biz
Email: email@boombooks.biz

Creator: Williams, Ron, 1934 - author

ISBN: 9780645182668

TABLE OF CONTENTS

IMPORTANT PEOPLE AND EVENTS

Queen of England	**Elizabeth II**
Prime Minister of Oz	**Gough Whitlam,**
Until December	
Leader of Opposition	**Malcolm Fraser,**
Until December	
Governor General	**Sir John Kerr**
The Pope	**Paul VI**
US President	**Gerald Ford**
PM of Britain	**Harold Wilson**

HOLDER OF THE ASHES:

1974 - 75	**Australia**	**4 - 1**
1975	**Australia**	**1 - 0**
1977	**England**	**0 - 3**

MELBOURNE CUP WINNERS:

1974	**Think Big**
1975	**Think Big**

ACADEMY AWARDS, 1975:

Best Actor	**Art Carney**
Best Actress	**Ellen Bernstyn**

PREFACE TO THIS SERIES

This book is the 37th in **a series** of books that I have researched and written. It tells a story about a number of important or newsworthy Australia-centric events that happened in 1975. The **series** covers each of the years from 1939 to 1975, for a total of 37 Titles.

I developed my interest in writing these books a few years ago at a time when my children entered their teens. My own teens started in 1947, and I started trying to remember what had happened to me then. I thought of the big events first, like Saturday afternoon at the pictures, and cricket in the back yard, and the wonderful fun of going to Maitland on the train for school each day. Then I recalled some of the not-so-good things. I was an altar boy, and that meant three or four Masses a week. I might have thought I loved God at that stage, but I really hated his Masses. And the schoolboy bullies, like Greg Fannell, and the hapless Freddie Ebans. Yet, to compensate for these, there was always the beautiful, black headed, blue-sailor-suited June Brown, who I was allowed to worship from a distance.

I also thought about my parents. Most of the major events that I lived through came to mind readily. But after that, I realised that I really knew very little about these parents of mine. They had been born about the start of the Twentieth Century, and they died in 1970 and 1980. For their last 20 years, I was old enough to speak with a bit of sense. I could have talked to them a lot about their lives. I could have found out about the times they lived in. But I did not. I know almost nothing about them really. Their courtship? Working in the pits? The Lock-out in the Depression? Losing their second child? Being dusted as a miner? The shootings at Rothbury? My uncles killed in the War? There were hundreds, thousands of questions that I would now like to ask them. But, alas, I can't. It's too late.

Thus, prompted by my guilt, I resolved to write these books. They describe happenings that affected people, real people. In **1975,** there is some coverage of international affairs, but a lot more on social events within Australia. This book, and the whole series is, to coin a modern phrase, designed to push the reader's buttons, to make you remember and wonder at things forgotten. The books might just let nostalgia see the light of day, so that oldies and youngies will talk about the past and re-discover a heritage otherwise forgotten. Hopefully, they will spark discussions between generations, and foster the asking and the answering of questions that should not remain unanswered.

The sources of my material. I was born in 1934, so that I can remember well a great deal of what went on around me from 1939 onwards. But of course, the bulk of this book's material came from research. That meant that I spent many hours in front of a computer reading electronic versions of newspapers, magazines, Hansard, Ministers' Press releases and the like. My task was to sift out, **day-by-day**, those stories and events that would be of interest to the most readers. Then I supplemented these with materials from books, broadcasts, memoirs, biographies, government reports and statistics. And I talked to old-timers, one-on-one, and in organised groups, and to Baby Boomers about their recollections. People with stories to tell came out of the woodwork, and talked no end about the tragic, and funny, and commonplace events that have shaped their lives.

The presentation of each book. For each year covered, the end result is a collection of short Chapters on many of the topics that concerned ordinary people in that year. I think I have covered most of the major issues that people then were interested in. On the other hand, in some cases I have dwelt a little on minor frivolous matters, perhaps to the detriment of more sober considerations. Still, in the long run, this makes the book more readable, and hopefully it will convey adequately the spirit of the times.

Each of the books is mainly Sydney based, but I have been **deliberately national in outlook**, so that readers elsewhere will feel comfortable that I am talking about matters that affected them personally. After all, housing shortages and strikes and juvenile delinquency involved **all** Australians, and other issues, such as problems overseas, had no State component in them. Overall, I expect I can make you wonder, remember, rage and giggle equally, no matter where you hail from.

BACKGROUND FROM 1973 AND 1974

By the start of 1974, our Prime Minister, Gough Whitlam,and his Labor Government, had been in power for about a year, and all were still relishing their task of fulfilling their promises set out so clearly in their election campaign.

All of these worthies had suffered for the past 23 years in the wilderness while the opposition Liberal Party had won election after election, and had glowed in having power in their hands.

But with the election win by Whitlam and Labor, a new bunch of politicians were free to strut their stuff. And strut it they did. They had been waiting for a long time, full of ideas and enthusiasm to change the world, and now they had an open book. With all the expertise that would be expected from a bunch of cowboys, with no experience in governing, they blundered into a wide range of overdue legislative activity that shook the nation.

Their very first act was to finally extract us completely from **the war in Vietnam**. They released from prison all the "conscies" who had refused to go to battle in Vietnam.

They let it be understood in the USA that we were definitely out of action in this sphere.

Whitlam's other Ministers were anxious to put their own ideas into place. **For divorce**, the same Rules were introduced across the nation. The only reason for seeking a divorce was now to become the "irrevocable breakdown of the marriage". and this took away much of the trauma of divorce hearings.

Civil marriages outside the Churches were **now** could now be officiated by women, **China** was **now** recognised, and trade with that country was henceforth encouraged. We all **forgot** about the War with **Japan**.

Death duties were payable to State Governments and to the Federal government. **Now,** both of these were abolished. This made a huge difference to the value of deceased estates.

The voting age was reduced to eighteen. Each of our two Territories were given **two** Senators in place of the existing ration of none. Commonwealth funding was extended to non-State schools. Early versions of a universal health scheme, Medicare was introduced. On and on went the benefits.

FLIES IN THE OINTMENT

But, the inevitable, but. There were consequences to all this largesse. In 1974-75, Federal spending by the Government rose by an astonishing 46 per cent, and the consequent blow-out in the national Budget, and inflation, contributed a fair deal to the troubles that lay ahead,

There was another problem that faced Labour in Government. After it won its election victory in 1972, it had a smallish majority in the House of Representatives, but **the Liberal Party still had a majority in the Senate,**

To Labour, this was often a comfortable situation because the House of Reps was the most powerful House **For example**, it could initiate new legislation whereas the Senate could not. And it could put new spending into the Budget, and again, the Senate could not.

This came to a head in early 1974. The Liberals, led by John Gorton, were holding up the passage of 62 pieces of legislation in the Senate. Whitlam used remote clauses in the Constitution to call for a double dissolution of both Houses of Parliament. And this in turn meant that nation-wide elections were held, and as part of the device, the backed-up legislation was passed through both Houses..

The result of the April, 1974 election reflected clearly the way that Australia thought about the efforts of the Labor Party over the previous last half-term. It had distributed largesse, it had undoubtedly made many social changes that were widely seen as welcome, it had ridden society of lots of conventions and rules that had stifled the population for decades.

Yet the results showed that nothing material had changed.

Labour still held the House, with even a small fall in Reps. The Senate also was much the same, with each Party still holding about half the seats, but more than likely it would be the Liberals that controlled it.

So it was a tied Parliament again. Granted, it had removed the back-log in 62 pieces of legislation, but the scene was set for a continuation of the stalling into the future. But apart from the numbers, the attitudes of the Parliamentary Parties remained more resolute than before. Labor would propose, and the Liberals would dispose. Is that the best way to run a nation?

It was still a hung Parliament. It seemed to be all set to repeat the whole performance again. How long could this go on, how many iterations could there be?

NON POLITICAL NEWS

After all that political excitement, we need to blink our eyes to see that there was still an entire society going about its business as though Parliament did not exist.

In the cities, the suburbs, and the country, life went on as normal. Men, and half the women, went off to work on a regular basis, came home to a good meal, and watched TV. On Sundays, there was usually the barbie, and few went to Church. Once a week, most families worried for a while about their mortgage payments, or their tax load. Occasionally some worried about changing jobs, though this was not yet common. In all, most people were comfortable and secure. Even for the disadvantaged there was a safety net, which though scarcely adequate, was better than in most other nets around the world.

But, **there were more flies loitering in this ointment.** After the April election, over a few months,Whitlam told the nation a few secrets. He told of the reality of existing and future inflation. He warned that this nation was trading at a loss with overseas nations. He said that, reluctantly, unemployment would rise, and austerity measures were certain to follow.

For the rest of the year, it turned out that he had called it right. In fact, the reality became even worse than forecast. The most crippling issue became the rise in inflation, so that by the end of the year, standard mortgage rates were set at 17 per cent. Imagine how the mortgagee in the suburbs felt repaying loans at that rate.

The second biggest issue was that **unemployment rose** as economic activity fell. Over the six months, the rate of unemployment doubled, and jobs became hard to get. **The secure nest in the background became much more of a worry.**

To make matter worse for the struggling Party, **a so-called scandal** engaged the Press. **It** concerned the now Treasurer Dr Jim Cairns. He had employed an attractive Philipina lady, named Juni Morosi as a type of Personal Assistant. The Press regaled its readers incessantly with innuendos of an affair between the pair. It was quite blatant about their affection for each other, and though they denied any intimacy, the Press pursued them relentlessly until the end of the year and beyond. We will find that they emerge into the news again next Year.

As a consequence of all this,, the Labor Party started to lose its electoral support. Poll after poll reported that people were getting fed up with bad news and expectations. This was right across the nation and across all classes. By December, it seemed obvious that if an election were called on that day, Labor would lose by a long shot.

TRACY AND DARWIN

But a great tragedy occurred instead. On Chrismas Day, revellers awoke to the news that Darwin had been devastated by cyclone Tracy. I gave a description of its effect in my 1974 book, so I will not repeat it here.

Suffice to say that every person in Australia was conscious of the tragedy as they ate their Christmas dinner that day, and as the news trickled through from damaged radio transmissions.

Coming in to 1975, the rehabilitation that followed was massive. The support that the nation gave to this made my heart glow.

Now, **we *are* ready to go into 1975. Fasten your seat belts.**

MY RULES IN WRITING

NOTE. Throughout this book, I rely a lot on re-producing Letters from the newspapers. Whenever I do this, I put the text in a different font, and indent it a little, and make the font somewhat smaller. **I do not edit the text at all**. That is, I do not correct spelling or grammar, and if the text gets at all garbled, I do not correct it. It's just as it was seen in the Papers.

SECOND NOTE. The material for this book, when it comes from newspapers, is reported as it was seen at the time. If the benefit of hindsight over the years changes things, then I **might** record that in my **Comments**. The info reported thus reflects matters **as they were seen in 1975.**

THIRD NOTE. Let me also apologise in advance to anyone I might offend. In a work such as this, it is certain some people will think I got some things wrong. I am sure that I did, but please remember, all of this is **only my opinion**. And really, **my opinion does not matter one little bit in the scheme of things.** I hope you will say "silly old bugger", and shrug your shoulders and read on.

JANUARY NEWS ITEMS

Buckingham Palace has released the names of Australians who have been awarded honours in the New Years Honours List. I am abashed to say that I hardly recognised any of them. This speaks more to my ignorance than to the character and deeds of the worthy recipients....

A few people I did recognise were the Dame of Sydney theatre, **Dorris Fitton**, and America's Cup Champion, **Syd Fischer**. Overseas, I knew of author **P G Wodehouse**, actor **Charlie Chaplin**, runner **Roger Bannister**, and Cricketer **Garfield Sobers**....

Famous Names, at the Australian Tennis Championship. **John Newcombe** won, beating **Jimmy Connors**. **Evonne Goolagong** won, beating **Martina Navratilova**. A good day for Australia.

Four men were convicted in Washington of conspiracy to obstruct justice. **All four were top officials** of the Nixon administration and played a big part in the Watergate scandal. Sentences for the four will be decided at a later date....

Nixon himself, as ex-President, was granted **immunity from prosecution** a few months ago.

Power shortages at homes and in the factories continue to frustrate people all over the nation. The typical situation developing over about four months. A small group of workers, say maintenance workers, repairing faults in equipment as they occur, go on strike for better conditions and more pay. The Union movement agree to support them, which means strike pay is given to them....

Blackouts occur in some areas, and increased as the faulty machines accumulated. Eventually, blackouts grow to about two hours a day in most homes, and occur one or two times a day....

Zoning is introduced, but it never works for long. More workers join the strike, and more Unions become involved. Out of the near-chaos, both management and Unions collectively start to compromise. Strikers all agree to resume work on the guarantee that the authorities hear their application for conditions and wages in the immediate future....

This occurs in every State, almost annually. Meantime householders and businesses suffer all the inconvenience and loss of profit.

An American **dare-devil** visited the Melbourne Show. His act included **riding a motor bike along a long narrow plank**, over the heads of an admiring crowd. But at his performance, the plank gave way, and he and his bike crashed to earth. Three people were injured. Of these, one small girl died....

Many activities, so carefully regulated **now** for safety reasons, were not regulated at all in 1975.

THE DARWIN DISASTER

The nation was still reeling after this disaster. Here was a frontier city without water, electricity, roads, ground transport, air transport, public transport, food, petrol, hospitals. It was in the most remote part of Australia, thousands of miles from anywhere. And half evacuated, and fully shocked. Law and order was dubious, most houses and public buildings were destroyed, and the wharves. The list of damages goes on and on.

Where do you start to fix it? Experts were just starting to work hard on this. Meanwhile the general population was doing everything it could. The easiest way was to donate money to the thousands of Relief Funds that sprang up.

All city newspapers started their own Funds, Banks did likewise, and so did clubs and sporting clubs, Churches, Unions, the local butcher. Entertainers gave performances and their cut went to Funds. Money poured in from everywhere.

But all this was a drop in the bucket, and the frantic efforts to rehabilitate, and re-build an entire city were as yet still on the drawing boards **Darwin would re-emerge, but it would take years.**

LETTERS ON DARWIN

Letters poured into the daily newspapers in all cities across the nation. Most of these were letters of appreciation from these who had somehow fled Darwin.

As they straggled into the Southern cities, they were met by all sorts of people and organisations who gave them food, clothing and accommodation, and in some cases cash, to get them by.

Letters, N Withnall. Late last Saturday my two children and I flew in to Sydney on an evacuation flight from Darwin.

We, and those with us, left behind a night of unforgettable terror, during which our homes and our whole way of life were torn and tossed away. We left behind days of anguished searching for relatives and friends; long nights spent without sleep trying to comprehend our shattered lives; hours, and in some cases days, of waiting in evacuation centres to bring our children to safety. We left behind us the unbelievable, nightmare ruins of our lovely tropical city.

We arrived in your City with few possessions and almost without hope, and the people of Sydney met us with open arms. On all sides gentle hands reached out to help us, to hold our tired children, to soothe us as we wept. All of us were moved beyond words. Indeed, there will never be words adequate to tell you all what your calm, efficiently organised and loving welcome meant to us in our weariness and sorrow.

I know that I speak for every Darwin woman who has carried her children to your City, and for our men who stayed at home, when I say that we thank you, with all our hearts.

Letters, D Boustead. I cannot express on paper my gratitude and thanks to those kind people who have given up their time and energy to help victims of the Darwin cyclone, in particular at Sydney Airport, where I was overwhelmed with the response.

I shall never forget their kindness.

Many other writers offered suggestions about what might be done to help the authorities, and people, get back to normal.

Letters, A Bode. Do the residents of Darwin, now so grateful to the Federal Government, realise that the insurance proceeds of their properties (except for some private residences) will be subject to capital gains tax? Also, that when the new Darwin Commission later resumes their land, the resumption price will likewise be subject to capital gains tax? In this case most residential sites will also be caught, because after December 25, 1974, they will not be the owners' "principal residences".

Letters, G Brodsky. Looking at films of Darwin after the cyclone havoc, one cannot help noticing the solidity of apparently almost unscathed public building of brick, steel and concrete, as compared to the flimsy structure of the razed private dwellings.

The planners of a rebuilt Darwin should seek and act on the advice of structural engineers. Building permits should be granted only for the erection of solid brick buildings appropriately reinforced with steel supports, with windows of shatter-proof glass and, possibly, without flat roofs resting on heavy beams, the collapse of which caused so many serious injuries this time.

The external walls, roofs, and windows should be capable of withstanding wind velocities of 252kmh. Since tropical cyclones originate at sea, the houses would need to be positioned in such a way that the edge of one corner of two brick walls faces in the direction of the sea and , like the bows of ships, would be most likely to break and withstand the maximum impact of a cyclone.

People are our most precious and irreplaceable asset, and must at all cost be protected better than anything else.

Anyone who does not subscribe to this view should have no say in the renaissance of Darwin

COMMENT. Some solutions may have been helpful. Some may not.

Letters, D Roberts. For what it is worth, may I suggest that the design of all buildings in cyclone-prone areas should be of igloo-type design built of reinforced concrete with plate-glass windows.

Being circular there would be no flat surface presented to the force of the wind thereby reducing the possibility of damage or destruction.

Multi-storeyed building could also be built circular presenting no flat surface to the elements.

Letters, G Pryce-Jones. I am no expert, but recalling the effects of the Blitz over Britain prompts me to suggest that when rebuilding Darwin, each home and establishment should have an underground shelter complete with an inlet and sanitation, and stocked with food and water, where the occupants could shelter when the "red alert" sounds again, as it undoubtedly will.

There could even be a siren so that if the shelter was buried under the wreckage of a house, the siren would indicate to rescuers that there were people there and the chance of loss of life and injury would be lessened.

Also a shelter would give residents the benefit of a temporary home while rebuilding went on.

This writer injects a timely word of caution into some calculations.

Letters, W Gold. Could the ailing Australian motor vehicle building industry revive itself permanently, and come to the aid of rebuilding hurricane-devastated Darwin, by diverting its designing and manufacturing resources to the mass production of scientifically designed houses produced on modified assembly lines and transported to Darwin in compact kit form for ease and speed of assembly?

The expertise in high-quality mass-produced houses gained by the Australian motor industry could be diverted at any time to meet housing needs elsewhere in Australia and overseas, building up a valuable export and domestic market.

Naturally such houses mass-produced for Darwin should be hurricane-resistant, and the computer-aided motor car design facilities could be of value in determining the parameters for such houses.

FUND RAISING FOR DARWIN

There were a multitude of ways of raising money for Darwin Funds. Here is an interesting suggestion.

Letters, R Granson. I am intrigued by the ingenuity of the various fund-raising schemes suggested for the relief of Darwin evacuees. The latest, by A Shelley, reminded me of a scheme introduced in England by my grandfather to raise money for the construction of communal playing fields in the 1930s.

The scheme was called the Odd Shillings and Pence Scheme and in principle worked like this: a donor would instruct the bank to transfer automatically from his or her cheque account to the appeal's account the odd shillings and pence remaining in the (positive) balance at the end of the accounting period. This was generally each month and the instruction was placed by means of a standing order.

Apparently, the idea was so successful that it had to be stopped soon after its inception and funds returned to donors. Whether this is true or not I don't know, but the playing fields were certainly developed.

The point about the story is that funds were raised on a regular basis for a continuing need in such a way that nobody but the recipient realised it was happening. I would think that there are many organisations in Australia which are almost indispensable from a social viewpoint but which depend upon a precarious income for their survival.

Comment. In today's world of 2025, there are probably problems in actually doing this. But the concept is interesting.

DARWIN VOLUNTEERS

Letters, L Johnson, Minister for Housing. I wish to express my disappointment at your coverage of the departure of 118 Trade Union volunteers to Darwin.

The caption *Volunteers get their 'shots' and $40 beer money* gives an unfortunate impression.

For the two weeks they will be in Darwin, the volunteers will be working without pay, except for $20 per week out-of-pocket expenses. To describe this as "beer money" is entirely wrong.

In fact, of the men who are personally known to me, many are non-drinkers.

I need hardly point out that these men will be engaged in arduous work in very difficult and uncomfortable conditions.

To give the impression that they are going to Darwin to make merry, is unworthy of the unselfishness of their generous gesture.

Comment. Interest and concern for Darwin remained strong in Society. In fact, even 50 years later, those whose lived through it can still remember in detail the sense of grief and frustration that everyone felt that Chrismas Day, as the dreadful news filtered through.

A COMMENT ON THE POWER STRIKE

This Letter summarises the opinions of most Letter writers about the cuts to electricity supply and the blackouts.

Letters, D Weeden. The Power Pantomime, the show with no heroes but plenty of villains. To NSW residents, this is not a premiere performance. Individuals and industries have worn it before and are wearing it again.

The effects on this occasion are likely, however, to have more serious repercussions than previously. Depressed economic conditions, difficulties for manufacturing industries and a projected 300,000 unemployed, provided an uninspiring backdrop to the present performance.

The initiated audience may well inquire what the Electricity Commission has done to reduce its dependence on a handful of maintenance workers since the last confrontation. Are the power workers really out of step with outside salaries and conditions? If they are, then why are they?

If the maintenance men have refused to do the job they are paid to do, they why have they not been retrenched? Who else in the community is paid for refusal to work?

The well-gilded cloak of responsibility at this time must rest on the shoulders of senior officials of the Electricity Commission and the responsible minister and they should wear it - to stand up to the power Unions, to use staff men if necessary, to maintain the State's assets (i.e. the assets of all Unionists), and if necessary to sack the few who refuse to do their jobs and let them wear it. As never before, "now is the time".

THE DERWENT DISASTER

The Tasman Bridge in Hobart in Tasmania joined up Eastern Hobart with Hobart proper. If you were to take away the bridge, it means a drive of 51 kms from the one place to the other.

On the night of January 5, a freighter, *Lake Illawara*, crashed into one pylon of the Bridge, veered off and hit another pylon. **300 meters of the bridge collapsed into the Derwent**, taking the ship to the bottom. Six crew members were killed by the impact, and six cars fell into the water, and their occupants drowned. It was an enormous tragedy.

The Prime Minister was in Paris at the time. He was distressed and angered by the news, and at a Press Conference, said "It is beyond my comprehension how any competent person could drive a ship into the pylons of such a bridge. But I have to restrain myself because such a person (the Captain) will surely find himself before a jury."

These remarks were badly received in Australia. Whitlam was seen as condemning the Captain of being guilty of some crime, long before any facts were known. Instead of a calm head in a time of crisis, the Prime Minister was seen as leveling accusations completely without foundations.

Editorials critised the words, the various maritime unions threatened nation-wide strikes, politicians from both sides laid the boot in. Even Jim Cairns, the Deputy Prime Minister, attacked the comments.

Within a day, Whitlam made a humiliating apology, He sent a telegram to the Captain, and apologised. He issued a brief statement that read "I withdraw unreservedly any imputation against the Captain of the Lake Illawara, and apologise to him."

Obviously some sort of deal had been concocted in the background, and the Captain did not respond in any way. But most Australians remembered the stress that the Captain must have felt from the remarks, and thought less of Whitlam as a result.

MORE ON THE DERWENT DISASTER

In Whitlam's initial Press conference, he included a snide reference to the air industry. He said that it was inconceivable that nautical and aircraft vessels were navigating irresponsibly.

Unions connected with the aircraft industry reacted heatedly. Pilots, for example, were amazed that they were connected in any way to the Tasman Bridge disaster. They sought an apology, which they did not get.

Whitlam, by such faux pas, was slowly building up groups that would remember him at election time.

WELCOME BACK, GOUGH

On return to Australia, he might well have wished he had stayed overseas.

He walked into the task of overseeing a nation racked by two disasters. Interest rates, and mortgage rates were about 17 per cent, the highest in the nation's history. Inflation was rife, and as a result, demands for wage increases, and strikes, were widespread. Thousands of workers were being laid off. Some of his Cabinet were restlessly talking about a coup, to be led by his Deputy, Jim Cairns, and while this did not occur, there was enough in it to ruffle feathers.

It seemed to most folk that he, and his Government, simply had no plan for a fix. Several Ministers made pleas during January for wage restraint, and Whitlam himself did so at the end of the month, but they hardly registered among workers whose living expenses were galloping. As one journalist asked "Are the lunatics in charge of the mad-house?"

Comment. It was all adding up for Whitlam. He was gradually losing the support of the people. Even to Labor supporters, he was still **a god**, but not **The God** of two years ago.

FEBRUARY NEWS ITEMS

The NSW Transport Department has decided that **school children must give up their seats**, on public transport, to adults. They can retain their seats if they pay full fare.

A **well-known nude beach**, Lady Game Beach, in Sydney, **was raided by police** this weekend. Three persons were arrested and charged with nudity. This was apparently a token raid, because many other nude people were ignored....

Police said they were forced to act because of a umber of complaints. The raid was seen as a reminder to the community that **nudity at beaches was a crime**, even at so-called nude beaches.

The President of the **South African Cricketing Association** was **refused a visa for entry** into Australia. His purpose here was to arrange a tour by a South African team later in the year....

The Labor Party is opposed to Australia playing **Rugby** with South Africa, because **their teams are selected on an apartheid basis**. In 1971-72 there were limited skirmishes with police when a South African Rugby team toured this nation....

Apparently, **the ban is now being extended to cricket**, and probably to all sports.

Do such bans really do much good?

The Federal Attorney, Lionel Murphy, has resigned. He will be appointed to the prestigious position of Judge in the High Court of Australia....

Murphy, with his two years in Office, was most **prolific in the amount of genuinely outstanding laws** that he produced. But he was a prickly person to deal with, so it could be that Whitlam would be pleased to see him go....

But little did he know that if Murphy was a headache **in** Cabinet, he would be a **full-blown migraine after he left**.

There has been talk in Canberra that the Australian Government is considering borrowing **a huge sum of money from Arab entities** who have become rich with petro-dollars from booming oil prices....

Such dealings by our Government would break many Treasury Rules. One hesitation would be that it is **not at all certain that the Arab dealers are trustworthy....**

Another hesitation is that the bulk of the money would go to satisfy the Minister for Minerals and Energy dreams for **vast mining adventures** to solve the nation' s balance of payments problems. Is that the gamble that we want to borrow money for?

Let us hope that there will be no further mention of this mad-cap idea.

SCOUT'S PROBLEMS WITH BOTTLES

The environment in the 2020's years has become a major force in the world. Green political Parties abound world-wide, and large development corporations tremble at their mention. This was not always the case.

Prior to the 1970s, the environment movement was almost invisible. Resistance to dangers was widespread but not at all organised.

Letters to the Editor was one avenue for protestors. This Letter below is typical. An individual, or small local organisation, raised its voice, was heard and forgotten.

Letters, R Manuell. The Scout Association has closed the bottle collection depot of the 1st Belrose Scout Group following complaints from local residents that the depot was a "dump" and a "fire risk".

Doubtless most people blame the Scouting movement for being untidy if not anti-social, when in fact the blame should lie with those few vandals who persist in using Scout bottle depots as general rubbish dumps.

The Scout Association, aided by its new Australian Scout Handbook, tries most earnestly to teach Scouts how to conserve resources and respect nature. Its outdoor code specifically charges Scouts to "correctly dispose of litter or rubbish" and "take an active part in conservation projects," among other things.

The community looks to the Scouting movement as a valuable source of capable, balanced citizens and leaders. May I appeal to those irresponsible few who dump their old refrigerators, tyres, beds, and builder's refuse at Scout bottle depots to give them a 'fair go' and help to show the next generation that what their Scouters are teaching is not really a load of old garbage.

From 1970, the realisation came that to make an impression, people **had to be organised into pressure groups**. And that is what happened. Green groups and Parties, and movements were slowly formed and grew, and now exert the substantial pressure that has become the norm today.

Comment. A good example of the mighty oak growing from a trivial acorn.

KEEP YOUR CLOTHES ON - OR ELSE

Lady Jane Beach is back in the news. Some of the arguments, for declaring selected beaches as being special, are trotted out in this Letter below.

Other arguments, opposing the nudity, say that there is nothing at all special about such beaches. Nude people are just nude people, and no matter where they are, give offense to many others.

Letters, J Disney, University of NSW. Unlike his predecessor as Minister of Police, Mr Waddy at least gave warning last Friday that he was ordering the police to make regular patrols of Lady Jane Beach and to take action against any one breaking the law. However, his actions must be criticised on several grounds.

First, the extent to which naked bathing at a well known and secluded nudist beach constitutes an offence is by no means clear in law. This uncertainty was aggravated last weekend when the police arrested three bathers who were emerging from the water, but ignored scores of other bathers who had been standing naked on the beach for some considerable time. In a just society criminal law must be clear, and be enforced fairly and consistently especially in relation to offences as serious as “indecent exposure”.

Second, Mr Waddy alleges that his action was forced upon him by the complaints of local residents. We need more details of these complaints before giving them much weight. With the possible exception of a few buildings in the military base, the nearest residences are in Camp Cove, which is at least a quarter of a mile away.

The only possible cause for complaint by these residents is the traffic congestion, which is due less to the attractions of Lady Jane than to those of Camp Cove itself. It is to be hoped that any such complaints from Camp Cove will be accorded neither more nor less sympathy than those from residents near racecourses, sports grounds and pubs.

Third, Mr Waddy alleges that the beach is a "focal point for perverts", that "prostitutes have been frequenting and soliciting at the beach" and that "the police have received numerous reports of disgusting acts". Perhaps the minister adopts a perverse interpretation of "perverts" and "disgusting acts", but conversations with many users of the beach lead me to doubt these allegations. Anyway, if they are true, the correct remedy is to obtain the evidence and bring the appropriate charge, not to make statements or take action to smear and prosecute the "dedicated sun-worshippers" for whom Mr Waddy professes less sympathy.

Comment. Another writer wrote a long Letter which said the crime was that wearing swim suits stopped the body from absorbing Vitamin C from the sunlight. We are thus as a society wasting this natural resource and **that** is the crime.

Yet another writer said that women in bikinis were a public eyesore, and should be banned from all beaches.

Second comment. It looked like a publicity stunt to me. That is, remove the three, but not charge them. But no. They were brought to Justice in Manly Court a month later. A slap on the wrist.

Third Comment. Every few years this matter of nudity at beaches pops its head up. And it blows over when the swimming season ends. No harm done.

A SMALL LESSON IN POLITICS

Whenever a Senator resigns from the Federal Senate, an immediate replacement must be found. The replacement must come from **the same State** as the departing Senator, and be appointed by the Premier of that State.

Senator Lionel Murphy was a Labor member, so **by convention**, it seemed that the incoming Senator would also be Labor. But that convention was only **that**, and it did not have to be implemented. It could be that a **Liberal** would be chosen by the NSW **Liberal Premier**.

That meant that the Liberals would gain one extra seat in the Senate, and that would take control of the Senate completely away from Labor. And that would mean that the Labor would be unable to get its proposals passed into law.

Would the new NSW **Liberal** Premier, Tom Lewis, defy convention and appoint someone favourable to the Liberals? The answer to that question was "**YES**", he most certainly would. **And this raised criticism from everywhere.**

Labor ripped into him to try to change his decision. Even some Liberal politicians attacked him, because they saw that if this situation was allowed to happen, it set a precedent and would be used against them in the future. **But he remained resolute**, and the NSW Liberal Cabinet supported him.

So, by the end of a month of intense bitter fighting, Murphy was definitely gone and, just as definitely, he was replaced by a Senator who would vote against Whitlam, and for the Liberals.

This was bad news for Whitlam's Labor Government that was really beginning to falter.

Comment. Even 50 years later, controversy remains over whether Lewis was justified in appointing a Liberal-voting person to a vacant Labor Senate seat.

At the time, in 1975, the issue was a really hot one. After all, as Whitlam pronounced, in dramatic terms, this action by Lewis was "an act of national sabotage."

Opinions differed.

The *Sydney Morning Herald* reported that the former Premier of NSW described Lewis as "mad", the prominent NSW Labor politician Neville Wran found the act "unbelievable". Even the Leader of the Federal Opposition, Mr Snedden, thought that Lewis should not do it. ,

The *SMH* took a different position. It pointed out that, several times in the past, the convention had been broken. **Does the refusal to change a convention now mean that no conventions would ever be changed?**

It pointed out that, just one year ago, Whitlam had broken with the same convention when he forced a double dissolution of Parliament and an election.

So the SMH was clearly in favour of Lewis.

But Senator James Mc Clelland did not agree with the *SMH.*

Letters, (Senator) James McClelland, Minister for Manufacturing. Your leader on Mr Lewis was remarkable, even in an anti-Labor newspaper, for its utter abdication of moral responsibility.

The really appalling thing about your leader was its cynicism; its sad proof that press proprietors will jettison any standards, any semblance of fair play, any pretence at rational discourse, when party prejudice is aroused.

The fact is that since 1949, under proportional representation, the balance in the Senate has been much more critical and the will of the voters consequently more vulnerable to attack. That is why the convention was adopted. That is why it has been observed without question for a quarter of a century by all political parties.

The *Herald,* in company with Mr Bjelke-Petersen and the fanatics of the Country Party, is alone among the newspapers of this country in its failure to recognise these simple facts and stand up for the elementary decencies of a civilised society. You ought to be ashamed of yourself.

Comment. Senator McClelland is clearly not in favour.

Second Comment. McClelland's answer hardly addressed the decision by Mr Lewis, and adds nothing to the situation. It was a rant against the *SMH.* But it does illustrate how fervid the Labor camp was over the matter.

Other writers had their say. Here is an opinion **supporting Lewis**.

Letters, J Sharp. The present pious bleatings of the Prime Minister and the Leader of the Government in the Senate about "convention" and "tradition" would be, at another time and in another place, something to be admired. However, the Prime Minister and the other members of his party could hardly expect their present utterances to be viewed in any other way than the last dying words of a frantic, frustrated and defeated Government.

From the very moment of the Labor Party's accession to power in December, 1972, the two principal figures in the present crisis mounted a deliberate campaign to demolish as many traditions which had been inherent in Australian life for decades as they could, in as short a time as possible. The traditional monarchical honours list was

> abolished with indecent haste; the traditional Premiers' conferences were abandoned (later, under the enormous pressure of mounting unemployment, to be resurrected); the traditional right of access of the States to the Privy Council has been threatened; even the traditional right of the Senate itself to exist has been questioned by the Government's idealists. The present hypocrisy is lamentable.
>
> And, as an afterthought, how highly the Prime Minister and Senator Murphy thought of "tradition" and "convention" when an Opposition senator was plucked from the chamber and dispatched on a diplomatic posting abroad for no other reason than the blatant attempt to gain control of the Senate. How different was that action, taken only nine months ago, to that which the brave Mr Lewis now proposes?

Most Letters that **supported Murphy's** leaving took one of two lines. **The first** was that this was a free country. A person could change jobs at will, and given Murphy was under no contract to stay in his present job, he must be free to change.

The second was that loyalty to the electors should stop him moving. They elected him on the expectation that he would serve a full term. Surely he should do that.

The answers were that, if he stayed, would the electors return the loyalty by guaranteeing to elect him again next time?

Both these opinions against Murphy seem flimsy to me.

Comment. In any case, the end result was that Murphy went, Whitlam ended up with one Senator less, and the Labor Government's hold on power seemed to be weakening.

Final Comment on Tom Lewis. Lewis had only just been appointed Premier in January of this year. He survived only until February next year. Then he lost in a landslide 22 to 11 vote, after losing a lot of support within the ranks over the Murphy affair.

MARCH NEWS ITEMS

A man walked into a bank in the centre of Sydney and demanded the teller give him money. He backed up his request by **producing a hand grenade** and pulling the pin out....

Another teller surprised the would-be robber, and chased him out of the bank. **Police were able to track the man down**, and arrested him. Tests proved that **the grenades were in fact live**, and exploded under testing.

The cost of bringing natural gas to Sydney will rise **by 30 per cent** in a few months. The gas will be piped from South Australia, and the cost rise will result from an increase in the price of construction. **From 10 Million Dollars to 250 Million.**

"At least 27 people were killed when **Israeli troops stormed a Tel Aviv waterfront hotel** which had been stormed by Arab terrorists." *SMH* front-page....

It is sad to say, that 50 years later, the situation between Israel and the Arabs still shows no sign of resolution. **Can there ever be?**

David Jones in December announced that it was the first store to **accept transactions using Bankcard.** The second corporation, Grace Brothers, said that it would do likewise in a few weeks....

Maybe credit cards could be here to stay.....

Though I personally doubt it.

Reports are that **jobs in Australia are being lost to overseas countries**. It seems that corporations are using more computers, and the availability of cheap operators overseas is encouraging them to place their punch-card operations there....

One reason given for the swap is that the **rate of pay here for overtime night-time work is prohibitive**.

An oil exploration company has announced a **major oil find off the North West Cape** in Western Australia....

This find proved to be very important for Australia and Western Australia. Since it started production, it has helped Western Australia with an ongoing level of prosperity much better than it would have otherwise had.

A 20-year-old teller was shot dead in a bank in Sydney's Bondi. The killer had **a white handkerchief covering his lower face**, rather like the movie outlaws in American B-Grade 1940's serials

The new Leader of the Opposition in Australia is Mr Malcolm Fraser. He defeated Billy Snedden in a Liberal Party Cabinet poll for leader. He is considered to be a much more capable Leader than Snedden, and **should prove a tough opponent for Geoff Whitlam**.

MORE JUNI MOROSI

Juni Morosi remains in the news. The printed Press and others are still pursuing her over the supposed fact that she and her former husband were on the edge of some allegedly fraudulent activity in the past. **Police had investigated this, and found there was no cause for action.**

Now she had been appointed by the Deputy Prime Minister, Jim Cairns, as his Personal Assistant. Sections of the Liberal Parliament called for her resignation because of the supposed adultery with Cairns.

Cairns refused to sack her, and the pair defiantly continued their public displays of affection towards each other. Behind all this chicanery, there were some persons, never publicly identified, **who were out to get Cairns**.

They hoped to unseat Cairns by exposing a scandal that would besmirch his reputation. The truth was that the public were not much interested in any adulterous affair in a Parliament that was notorious for such.

Cairns responded to the latest round of criticism of Morosi in his usual vigorous manner, and the whole cycle started again. Meanwhile, the antagonism between Whitlam and Cairns grew apace.

I will keep you posted if anything changes.

NAUGHTY, NAUGHTY CHILDREN

During February, there were many angry scenes in Federal Parliament over Mr Lewis's decision. Both Houses suffered from angry outbursts by Members, shouting across the aisle was the norm, verbal abuse and other signs of contempt reached crisis point. So much so that the Speaker in the House, Jim Cope, resigned. The same was true for the NSW State Parliament, where manners and decorum went out the window.

Readers did not like this.

Letters, (Mrs) C Jones. As an Australian citizen, I am appalled by the decline in the standard of debate in Federal Parliament. This has reached an all-time low, with the spectacle of so-called intelligent men on both sides indulging in personal insults and invective. Scoring points off your opponent seems to be the substitute for reasoned argument.

Despite avid assurances of our "intelligence" at election time when vote-catching is at a premium, it soon becomes patently clear that politicians have no respect for the electorate at all. We are stupid.

Australians concerned for their country must be very disturbed by the obvious lack of responsibility shown by our representatives. The downhill slide must have repercussions eventually on the parliamentary system as a whole.

Letters, E Haines. I forced myself to undergo a sadistic form of mental torture this week by listening to Parliament during questions without notice.

I am ashamed of my elected countrymen. If this was a sample of the usual proceedings during this period, I can only ask when do our elected parliamentarians, of all political colours, intend to get on with the business at hand instead of indulging in constant "little squabbling boys" slanging matches?

Comment. Any viewer or listener to the daily broadcast of Parliament at the time, and **every day since**, would agree with these two readers

Even today, in 2025, **it seems as if the hatreds of Question Time are written into the Constitution**. No Minister must ever answer a direct question. Every **Speaker** must be fully biased towards the Government of the day. Members must be warned several times with no consequences. Shout out and cat-call at will.

It is a situation we have lived with for many years.

Comment. Usually, I can make a suggestion as to why something silly happens. But this time, I cannot even get started.

HIGH COST OF IMPORTS

Letters, J Burman. Not only are Australians unable to manufacture commodities at a world price, they are unable even to import them at a world price. I have wondered why a paperback book, published and printed in England and retailed there for 30 pence (about 53 cents) should cost $1.20 here.

Amateur photographers may wonder why a roll of colour-slide film should cost Two Pounds 10 ($3.70) in England but $6.45 here. Collectors of fine English china may wonder why they have to pay almost three times as much for their pieces as an English collector. The same comparisons apply to almost anything else you can think of. At these prices it would be cheaper to wrap and mail individual items from England than buy the same bulk-shipped goods in Australia.

THE FAMILY LAW BILL

One of the many good things that Lionel Murphy left behind, as he passed on to the High Court, was the Family Law Bill. This was near, after many revisions, and Amendments, and arguments from a wide section of the community. It was to be presented to Parliament via a conscience vote, hopefully reducing Party influence.

The Bill has too many provisions for me to elaborate. But to mention only **four**. **First**, it made divorce laws uniform across the nation. No longer would people be able to change provisions simply by hopping across the borders between States.

Second, it made divorce into **a no-fault proposition**. No longer would both parties be called upon to tell the Court that they were blameless and the other party was a villain. No longer would private detectives jump out of closets with cameras flashing to provide evidence of adultery.

Third, disputes over payment for alimony and family support were to be simplified and more considerate, and depend on actual situations rather than ritualised formulae.

Fourth, in adultery situations, the third party was called a co-respondent. Previously, co-respondents were most often named by the courts, and their behaviour investigated in public very closely. It was generally an embarassing experience for all concerned. **The new no-fault divorce stopped this practice.**

But there were many other provisions and it was generally agreed that **the nation was a better place for them**.

Some few opinions are cited below.

Letters, J Watkin. I cannot let Archbishop Loane's letter pass without comment.

My credentials for entering into this endless argument can only be based on my very bitter experiences in the Family Law Division of the Supreme Court.

The point which seems to have been missed - except by those who have witnessed and experienced the application of the present law - is that persons seeking a divorce are not criminals.

For instance, **under the present law**, a woman, whose husband has deserted her and, for reasons of his own, finds himself unwilling to consent to a divorce, will leave his wife with a number of choices under the present system. They are:

* She can wait in loneliness, misery and isolation, in the hope that her husband may return to her.

* She can wait for three years, and then seek a divorce on the grounds of his desertion.

If she suspects that there may be “another woman,” she can (if she has the money) engage a private inquiry agent in the hope of ferreting out the errant husband in an act of adultery.

* Or (God forbid, but this action is prevalent now among the young and educated, who will not involve themselves in the present outmoded system) admit falsely that she has committed adultery, and allow the husband to divorce her.

* Enter into an arrangement whereby the husband falsely admits adultery. (Again a prevalent practice, well-known to the Divorce Law Reform Association.)

Adultery is still the fastest method by which a divorce may be obtained, providing both parties will co-operate. However, supposing the wife does not wish to become involved in such collusion, and that she obtains proof of her husband's adultery, in nine cases out of 10, because the husband has been placed in an embarrassing social position, and because he fears scandal, disgrace and financial ruin, he retaliates in every possible fashion. He experiences rage, indignation, guilt, embarrassment (in the eyes of his children and society) and fear, and, finally, if he has not seen a solicitor previously, he hot-foots it very smartly to the toughest one he can afford.

With the help of the law, under the present system all hell breaks loose.

In this situation, the wife has no protection. The husband is assisted by law to make his wife's life as unbearable as possible by refusing alimony (until forced to after horrible courtroom procedure), by hounding her day and night in the hope that he might find her in some compromising situation, and in general the whole situation gets out of hand.

The emotional factor in divorce must be removed. Once a "clean" divorce is granted - well they can always marry again, can't they?

Or would the Archbishop refuse them that as well?

Letters, C Lynam, President; A Bailey, Executive Director, YWCA It is our view that, in terms of human relations, the proposed Family Law Bill 1974 is a great improvement on the Matrimonial Causes Act, which it is designed to replace.

We regret the extreme polarisation of views expressed by concerned groups in the community that consider the bill all bad or all good and obscure many of the improvements.

We particularly welcome the provisions that treat the participants in a marriage as equal partners with no discrimination on the basis of sex.

We are glad that the concept of matrimonial fault is eliminated and that the 14 existing grounds for dissolution of marriage are replaced by a single ground of irretrievable breakdown of marriage.

We are heartened that human dignity will be respected by the privacy and the general availability of the services of the Family Court.

Letters, E Quinlan. The Rev Fred Nile, director of the Festival of Light, has every right to speak for himself and those who adhere to his beliefs. For me, although raised and educated in a Christian faith, his beliefs are meaningless.

Mr Nile's five modern "heresies" are all perfectly reasonable propositions. I support them. If the Festival of Light feels that the vast majority of

Australians share its views, it is mistaken, as is evidenced by recent polls on abortion and divorce.

I have studied the proposed Family Law Bill in detail, together with proposed amendments. I consider the bill should be passed in its present unamended form. As a woman I am concerned about its effects on members of my sex, and a study of the bill makes it clear it is just both to women and men. I find no insult to my sex in it.

Concerning breakdown of marriage, a marriage has broken down if one of the parties seriously wants to get out, and if one party is of this mind for 12 months, then the marriage has certainly irretrievably broken down. It does not take 12 months to know that you can no longer endure living with someone you no longer love or want.

So far as maintenance is concerned, the bill makes adequate provision for those whose need is genuine. No woman should expect a bread ticket for life merely because she marries.

Mr Nile's comments on easy divorce providing a kind of substitute prostitution are too ridiculous for comment. His inference that women and children will be the victims of the bill when passed is an obvious scare tactic aimed at women voters. I hope they will not be fooled by it.

Letters, A Bartlett. I object to Archbishop Sloane's that he, along with the Rev Alan Walker, Cardinal Freeman and other "responsible churchmen" are expressing the views on divorce of the Christian community as a whole.

As a Christian lay person, it has continually been my experience that many leaders of our Churches are expressing views that the "ordinary" Christian cannot endorse.

I believe the day has passed when people, out of fear and guilt, gullibility believed everything our Archbishops, Cardinals, etc. said, because we, the people, live in the world and not a plastic bag, and we have to face the realities of life, including the problem of marriage breakdown.

Marriage and religion are strongly based on people's emotions, therefore making every situation in these areas of our lives completely individual. Many lay Christians see the Family Law Bill, particularly the clause relating to irretrievable breakdown in marriage, as a major breakthrough in ridding our society of laws on moral questions in which someone has to be guilty.

Comment. The proof that this Bill met many of the needs of society at the time is that it still stands, with much unchanged and unchallenged, 50 years later.

SMOKING IS A HOT ISSUE

Letters, P Gracie. My wife is a patient in The Royal North Shore Hospital, where she has undergone major surgery. Her ward is not air-conditioned and the only fresh air ventilation is that provided on fine days by open windows. On still, hot days she and the other non-smokers are obliged to share the cigarette fumes exhaled by the lady smokers and their visitors which gather in an ugly grey haze above the beds.

How can the practice of smoking in such a place as a hospital, where the air is otherwise hopefully antiseptic, be tolerated? Surely in a hospital the rights of the non-smokers not to have their well-being assaulted by others ought to prevail.

What kind of logic informs the hospital authorities who wisely ban the consumption of alcohol by patients, which can only harm the consumer, yet permits smoking, which harms both smokers and non-smokers alike?

Nurses are not permitted to smoke on duty, so why should not the same rule apply to patients? I imagine that hospital rules are made by doctors, who ought to be better informed on the nature of health hazards than others.

Why have they got a blind spot in the case of smoking? If the doctors won't speak up, perhaps the nurses should. It would certainly make their work more pleasant.

Letters, (Dr) N Packham, RPA Hospital. Mr Gracie might reasonably imagine that hospital rules are made by doctors, but, in fact, they are made by individual hospital boards which are largely composed of non-medical people. Not all the members of these boards are convinced that "smoking is a health hazard."

However, the Royal Prince Alfred Hospital Board, acting on the advice of the medical staff, had erected in the wards, and other public places of the hospital, signs requesting people not to smoke. The effort was to little avail, and hapless patients share the grey haze that Mr Gracie encountered.

The hospital administration seems unable to enforce prohibition, and nurses and ward staff, on attempting to obtain co-operation from hospital visitors, are not infrequently met with truculent refusal or even proffered violence from the smoker who is intent on preserving his "rights."

If the Health Commission cannot compel observance and enforcement of its code on smoking, who can? Health is a Government responsibility. It used to cost $4 to spit in a Government tram. Surely the fee for smoking in a Government public hospital should be no less.

APRIL NEWS ITEMS

In 1953, New Zealander **Edmund Hillary**, and his Sherpa guide, reached the top of Mount Everest, and **celebrated this stirring event with cakes and oxygen**. **Hillary was seen by the world as a hero**, and spent his next 30-odd years raising funds to develop hospitals and shelters for the impoverished Sherpas....

Now, **sadly, his wife and his child were killed in a plane crash** when they flew in to visit him in Katmandu. The world will mourn this great loss to Sir Edmund.

Our Governor General, John Kerr, got married for a second time in a private ceremony. Lady Kerr has a distinguished academic and employment record. She will need much fortitude in the difficult months ahead for Sir John....

A few brave commentators hoped that maybe this marriage would reduce his consumption of alcohol, which they considered to be more than it should be for a man in his position.

Victoria and South Australia have removed capital punishment from their schedules of penalties.

An elderly man **was found guilty of shop-lifting cigarettes** to the value of six Pounds in a Brisbane Court. A psychologist stated that he was old and very sick, and not of criminal intent. **The Crown decided not to proceed**....

Comment. A few commentators suggested that the fact that the gentleman was **the former Commissioner of Queensland Police** may have influenced the Court.

Australia will take in 200 child refugees from Vietnam. These children are left-overs from the war there....

But they serve as a reminder that, although we were no longer involved, the war in Indo China was still being fought. **Basically, Communists versus the rest, with nationalism thrown in for luck.** The location of hostilities may have moved from Vietnam generally to Saigon, but **the carnage was still the same**.

NSW Parent bodies for school children are now **seriously advocating that the cane should not be used in future in schools**. The practice is not used in many schools, but it may be used where it is considered prudent. Girls' schools never use it, but **some boys still enjoy the pleasure of six-of-the-best**.

140 war orphans from Vietnam, flying to the USA, were killed when their plane crashed. None survived.

INTRODUCTION OF MEDIBANK

The medical industry is facing an uncertain future. The Federal Government has announced that a new system of medical insurance will come into effect from July 1. The plan is being redrafted at the moment, so few details are available.

Insurance at the personal level is not much used by Australians. Some have personal insurance against death, more have building insurance, a few have contents insurance. But most see insurance as a losing bet where **other** people will suffer a catastrophe that will never befall **them**. The policies that do exist are underwritten by insurance companies, guilds, Unions, co-ops, benevolent societies, and form an industry that is virtually unregulated and scarcely under scrutiny by regulators.

Now, **on July 1st, every adult in the nation will be insured medically under a giant single policy underwritten by the Federal Government**. The premium will be paid generally from wages and salaries, and no one will be exempt from some payment. Every person in the nation will be covered to some extent, and that means that the young support the older until they themselves become elders.

The medical industry is vital to Australia. Every doctor, every nurse is part of it, and so too are service providers such as psychologists and technicians and dentists and opticians. And patients are obviously vitally affected, so too are institutions such as hospitals. The list goes on and on.

With so much at stake, speculation is running riot. Would the new system be similar to UK nationalisation? Would that mean all doctors become government employees? Would all fees be abolished, or only for a subset of services? Would dental fees be included?

How do specialists fit in? Would X-rays be charged for? Drugs from pharmacists? This list **also** goes on and on.

Letters, L Hoare, President, Aust. Assn. of Surgeons. I wish to bring to the attention of your readers the appalling situation applying between surgeons and the Australian Government concerning the introduction of conscripted medicine - Medibank - from the First of July.

We have been ignored by the Government and given no details of the scheme.

We must assume, however, it is the Government's intention to totally phase out private surgical care - a most retrograde step which we will oppose totally in the interests of our patients and of medicine as a whole.

The woeful situation is that Mr Hayden plans to socialise medicine by stealth; to sacrifice private and intermediate surgical treatment on the altar of political expediency.

Representatives of the Australian Association of Surgeons from all States met in Sydney recently. At this meeting it was decided to seek a deputation to Mr Hayden to clarify his intentions.

In the meantime, this Association strongly urges every Australian to maintain private health insurance if they want their surgical and hospital care to be more than the mere shuffling of numbers through a bureaucratic maze of confusion.

The meeting decided that any section of the Medibank scheme found to be against the interests of patients will be opposed by the full strength of the 1400 members of this Association.

Letters, Dr J Prior. Through your columns I would like to alert pensioners to the implications of Medibank.

Under our present health system, they only have to sign a voucher to receive free treatment. When Medibank is launched there will be no more vouchers to sign. Pensioners will be given an account just like any other patient. They will have to fill in a claim form and present the account and form to the Medibank agency. Medibank will only pay 85 per cent of their account. The pensioner will have to pay the rest out of his own pocket.

Under the present health system, the pensioner receives free treatment; under Medibank he will have to pay for part of it himself. What a colossal Labor Government confidence trick. They hope to economise by imposing this charge on pensioners so that they won't visit their doctors so often.

Pensioners, organize yourselves now so that you can demand the free treatment the Government is promising. Don't be fobbed off with 85 per cent of your doctor's account. Demand that the Government refunds you 100 per cent.

Comment. The confusion is apparent. But it is important to realise that they portend a great deal of strife is ahead. There are about 50 organisations in the medical industry that are capable of fighting like mad when their livelihoods are threatened. None of these will lie down and accept what the Government will propose if it threatens their income. How the Government tries to do this will be a matter of much argument over the next three months. **And after that, I expect.**

WRITE A *LETTER TO THE HERALD*

The man and woman in the suburbs and country had the usual burdens to bear. The everyday irritations that beset us all. But in case you do not know what I mean, I will include a few that were annoying 1975 writers.

Letters, J McDermott. The Australian Government poses as being in favour of women's liberation and can point to a number of initiatives which at least demonstrate token respect for the aims of that movement.

I have always understood that one of the basic tenets of women's liberation was that a woman's value was not judged by her looks or her years. In view of this, it is with increasing scepticism that I observe recent Government female appointees appear, without exception, to be young and attractive. It is to be hoped that the Government reaches its recruitment ceiling before the ACT is denuded of the obviously limited number of potential employees able to satisfy the new criteria.

Letters, (Dr) A Forbes, MP. I refer to your sound editorial, pointing out the position we are in as a result of the Government's lack of interest in, and failure to provide funds for, defence.

Your statement in a final throw-away sentence that "the Opposition seems as little concerned as the Government" is not correct. In a series of speeches and statements over many months both in Parliament and outside I have, on behalf of the Opposition, stated and documented that concern, and indicated the measures which we will implement when we are able to form a Government. Indeed,

I was even taken to task editorially recently by a Melbourne newspaper for indulging in "political hyperbole," so strongly did I express our concern.

As I have said on numerous occasions, the longer the Government's neglect of defence continues, the more dangerous the situation becomes, because it will take longer to rectify. The manpower the services are losing in such large numbers and the equipment that is not being ordered or replaced all have very long lead times. There is no doubt in the Opposition's view, that the Government is heavily mortgaging Australia's future security.

Letters, P Newman. Many years ago I saw an old play entitled The Ghost Train, which was, of course, a fable. However, it seems that ghost trains run today in New South Wales.

It all happened this way. A relation of mine, returning to academic duties in Armidale, booked on the 8pm train from Hornsby to that city last Saturday. His wife, on hearing this news, checked in Armidale at the local station to be told that there was no such train. Mind you, my relation had booked at the Railways Office in Martin Place and had observed various checks being carried out to ensure that the train was running and that he could have a sleeper. When his wife told him the news, he rang Hornsby Station. An anonymous official told him that the train was certainly running. Foolishly, he decided that those in Armidale knew not what they were doing; after all he had a ticket issued with the full authority of the Public Transport Commission of New South Wales, which said there was a train.

After half an hour's wait on Saturday night at Hornsby Railway Station, he went to see the stationmaster. That official was in no doubt - there was no train. He bothered to volunteer that "this is happening too often." So passeth the ghost train.

Letters, N Pollock, Principal, Rosehill Public School. Thousands of city and country residents are visiting the Royal Easter Show. How many of those who stream through the gates realise that the **children of showmen** suffer possibly the greatest degree of educational deprivation in the community?

As a school principal who, for periods of short duration, enrols these unfortunate itinerants, I am appalled by the disadvantages under which these children labour. From week to week the child is confronted with a strange school, a strange teacher, an unfamiliar educational programme, and periodically with an entirely different school system. Is it any wonder that, in the majority of cases, interest is lacking, performance is poor, attendance is irregular, and the potential of many young Australians remains undeveloped?

The problem is compounded by the fact that many showmen travel interstate, and State Governments disclaim continuing responsibility. It would appear, therefore, that the Australian Minister for Education must consider ways, such as the provision of staffed mobile schoolrooms on show circuits, whereby these children shall enjoy equal education opportunities.

THE WAR IN INDOCHINA

When the fighting stopped in Vietnam two years ago, the battle lines at that date became the new boundaries between North Vietnam and South. So, when in January this year they started to war again, the South held only a few cities and strips of territory along the coast.

As this war went on, the battle in the Australian Press continued as well. Old opponents from the trenches of the First Vietnam War re-emerged and continued their polemics of a few years ago. None of them apologised and said that they were wrong. No, indeed, they all said that they had been right, and history had proved that. And none of them had a solution to the problem, whatever that might have been.

I enclose a few Letters. You can see that all writers are passionate, sincere, still convinced that they were right. They all wish to make things different, but have no realistic suggestions to offer.

It was as if we were in a time trap, and nobody had learned anything from the past decade

Letters, (Rev) J Wyndham. I write with a mixture of anger, sorrow, shame and frustration as I consider the situation in South Vietnam at this time.

My anger is directed to those who beguiled the Australian people in the days of the Moratorium movements, persuading popular (?) opinion to press for a withdrawal of our forces from South Vietnam. I have waited in vain for the leading members of the present Government, the so-called Christian leaders and the "intellectuals" to admit that they were wrong.

My sorrow stems from the reports of thousands fleeing from the "liberators" in fear and agony. That sorrow becomes greater as I think of Vietnamese nationals whom I met while serving for a short time as a chaplain to the Australian forces....

All this leads to my frustration, as I find myself seemingly unable to do anything. I read the statements of people like M A Fox and G Pawsey and I wonder how they can be so blind and so gullible in the light of Korea, Hungary and Czechoslovakia and now Vietnam. And like D Thomas, I long to hear the leader of the

1970 protest movement, Jim Cairns, explain the situation to us.

About 500 Australian soldiers died in South Vietnam and, thanks to the so-called "pacifists," the Communist supporters and sympathisers, the humanist idealists, and the many who were unthinking and perhaps even selfish, they appear to have died in vain. While they were there, while the other "free world" forces were there, the people who did not want Communism had a chance to choose their own way of life. It is a chance which is quickly being denied.

Dr Cairns, Mr Fox, G Pawsey - why don't you and your friends and supporters admit that you were wrong, that you still are wrong? Why don't you call upon Hanoi to go back to the north, and to cease sending military supplies to the Vietcong? Why won't you let the people of South Vietnam have a chance to enjoy the kind of freedom that you still have despite yourselves?

Letters, K McLean. I wish to add my voice to the protests against the present situation in South Vietnam. My sympathy goes to the refugees, the homeless and the wounded, but particularly to those Australians who lost sons in Vietnam.

As a neutral and peaceful citizen of Sydney, I want to know where those people who objected so strongly by letter and demonstration to the presence of Australian and Allied forces in Vietnam a couple of years ago, have gone. The group of several hundred who marched down George Street one sunny afternoon chanting “One, two, three four, we don’t want your ----- war,” or the lad who was sitting on the Cenotaph in Martin Place and claimed he had every right to do so if he so desired. My comment to him was: “If you want to sit on the Cenotaph it’s OK, I suppose, but I request you sit somewhere else, and if some ex-serviceman who saw his mates die so that you may be free to express your personal beliefs comes along and breaks your neck - please don’t complain.”

The attitude of those people worries me, and no doubt worries thousands of other people in my age group.

War is a dirty business, no matter whose side you are on. Here’s to a quick victory to the Commies. May they end the misery and suffering soon. Then where do they go?

Letters, J Tinkler. So Thomas Keneally, the novelist, has at last been convinced that his actions and the actions of others who sponsored Moratorium ads did nothing to bring peace in Vietnam. On the contrary, all that was achieved was to give further encouragement to the Vietcong and North Vietnamese for a full-scale invasion of the South.

> At least we can say that when we were involved together with the United States and other allies, the peoples of South Vietnam felt reasonably secure - the kids were happy, large-scale areas were continually being declared safe from further Vietcong intervention and, given time, we could have consolidated and made secure additional areas of South Vietnam for the peoples of South Vietnam.
>
> But thanks to Mr Keneally and his associates we are now witnessing one of the greatest massacres of women and children this world has ever seen.

In April, after a few months of the familiar pattern of "win a few battles and lose a few", the North triumphed and Saigon and South Vietnam capitulated on April 30.

But in those four months, refugees poured out of the South, and they really picked up as the realities of living under Communist rule sank in. They left the country by all available means, and so started the exodus of **"Vietnamese Boat People"**.

For the next year, they scrounged whatever small vessels they could and took to the ocean. They ended up all over the world, including parts of Australia. Generally, they were given refugee status, and were welcomed, without visa complications. Australia took in about 2,000.

Of the 2 million persons who left Vietnam as boat people, half a million died at sea.

MAY NEWS ITEMS

The NSW country city of **Wagga Wagga** has arranged for **a "shoot" covering 16 blocks of the city**. The aim is to rid the city of **thousands of starlings** that are despoiling that part of the city. The dead carcases will be carried away on especially arranged garbage trucks.. ..

The City Council claims that **the cull will benefit both the people of the City and the starlings....**

As yet, the **starlings have not responded to this latter claim.**

An English family of five **migrated back to England** after spending five years in Australia. **They lasted 24 hours in England** and have now departed from there, on the way to Australia....

They explain that Britain is unchanged and is **as dead as ever**. No jobs, no sunshine, no open spaces is their summary.

The first major poll of electors, since Fraser assumed leadership of the Opposition, shows **that 68 percent of voters think that his presence will improve the prospects** of a Liberal win.

The President of the ACTU will set up **union-backed petrol retail businesses** to compete with existing retail costs. Prices will be about 20 percent off....

This is **the third of Hawke's ACTU business ventures**. The others are Bourke's ACTU store, based in Melbourne. And ACTU New World Travel....

These are out of character for the ACTU or an ACTU leader. Does it mean that the very centre of the Trade Unions, the ACTU, is about to enter the world of Capitalists, and adopt a Liberal viewpoint?

The Health Ministers in all States agreed to issue a **health warning on the packets of all cigarettes packets sold**. The Warning will say "Warning. Smoking is a health hazard."

A number of police officers are employed daily to supervise traffic crossings outside schools in Sydney. Now these officers will return to normal duties as they are **replaced by special appointees in their lolly pop duties....**

Specially outfitted, and carrying appropriate signage issued by the Government, **they will patrol crossings outside 70 schools each day**.

The shoot of starlings at Wagga Wagga was not a success. The blocks of buildings in the City Centre were closed off, and registered shooters blazed away for precisely 30 minutes. Only about 150 were killed. The plain trees throughout the area provided too much protection from the shot-gun pellets....

But, you will be pleased to know, **the shooters will return for a half-hour next week**.

BACK TO OZ POLITICS

Yes, Australia is still here. But, economically it seems to be in worse condition month after month. Interest rates at the end of March were 17.6 per cent! Unemployment was the highest on record. Every commentator and Letter writer seemed to point to some aspect of the economy that was gradually getting worse.

Letters, P Kennedy. The announcement that a record number of working days were lost through industrial disputes in Australia during 1974 adds another dimension to the already frightening list of records established by the Whitlam Government.

These are records which are literally milestones on the road to economic disaster and which collectively constitute a scathing indictment against the Whitlam Government - records such as record inflation, record unemployment, record interest rates, and record rates of personal taxation.

Even more frightening, however, is the speed at which this transformation of the economy was brought about; a transformation which in itself must constitute yet another record in so far as the Labor Government has managed to accomplish in a little more than two years what successive Liberal-Country Party Governments could not accomplish in 23 years.

Comment. Importantly, the polls were showing that Labor was losing favour with the working class. Not that there was a complete switch by voters to the Liberals. But just a few points every month, enough to make Labor wonder whether it was under threat if this trend continued.

SPARE THE CHILD AND SPOIL THE SCHOOL

Should the cane or strap be used in schools? It is an old argument. And it is surfacing again. Most parents advocate a ban, but hedge and say that, when necessary, stronger discipline is acceptable. When pressed they talk about suspension, and duck the question.

The four Letters below are typical of responses.

Letters, E C Dicker (Principal) and members of the executive of St Marys High School, Sydney. The executive of St Marys High School is appalled at the unrealistic attitude shown by the Council of Parents and Citizens' Associations to school discipline.

The council's reforming zeal does not stop at attacking the use of corporal punishment. It seeks to ban all punishment in schools, including detention and "verbal assault" and "the various forms of humiliation which are now practised."

Are the councillors suggesting that they have never smacked their children, or "verbally assaulted" them, or given them a "hiding?"

Would parents accept the school suspending their child from school? Would they be prepared to have teachers refuse to have their child in the class because of rudeness, uncouthness and downright abuse of the teacher? Surely the teacher also has some right to expect not to be subject to abusive, invective and obscene language? After all the teacher has up to 40 years to "put up" with this type of child and should not be expected to tolerate what some pupils can do, and have done.

If the council wishes to be constructive, why not press for the right of the school to suspend or expel pupils who breach the bounds of propriety and, as is done in some American States, take legal action against the parents whose children are not then kept at home or admitted to another school.

We agree it might also be constructive if re-entry to school was made easy for those who later on realise they made a mistake, but while they are about it, how about pressing the right of children to say "we've had enough school and want to leave" no matter if the age be 12 or 13 or 14 years.

Given these reforms and the realisation that secondary education is not a right but a privilege to be earned, then there would be no need for any other disciplinary measures and no need for blazoned headlines, Bid to Ban the Cane.

Letters, D Reeve, Principal, Cambridge Park Public School. It is saddening to read of proposals to legislate to prevent children from being caned, kept in or scolded in school. No doubt it is part of the present campaign to undercut and control the authority of school principals.

Every parent has the right to demand that his own child should not be caned or detained and to protest when his child is scolded. Should he, however, also have the right to determine what is to happen to other people's children?

In these days of deserted wives, it is commonplace for a distraught mother to come to a principal and ask for help in controlling a wayward child for what he does at home, let alone school. There are many occasions when parents have taken their children to the local police for advice only to be told to approach the school.

It is by no means unusual for a gang of young bullies to set upon a younger defenceless child and beat him up on the way home from school. If repeated warnings fail to stop the practice, what does the Parents and Citizens' Federation suggest should be done?

In a large school there are inevitably a few children who have no intention of learning anything but who enjoy being disruptive and aggressive and, by daily confronting their teachers, effectively prevent other children from learning.

The P and C Federation suggests using a remedial teacher (whatever that is). But suppose our plucky little rebels tell her to "-------." What then?

There were others who favoured a tougher line.

Letters, Sam Hordern. I was a teacher for 40 years, and saw schools use every conceivable method to deal with delinquency. Most of these had a positive effect, but in quite a few cases, had no effect or even heightened the delinquency.

Once it reaches a certain level, the school should realise that its job is to teach, not police offenders. **You can't do both.** The school or teacher who tries do both **destroys the chances of every other child in classes**.

The remedy is to realise **tha**t, and separate the delinquent from the class. **Get rid of the delinquent.** Use the Police, or Law Courts, or expulsion, whatever is the most convenient. But get rid of the offender for ever. Get on with teaching those who are willing to learn. And let those who are paid to deal with delinquents get on with their jobs.

Execute this policy with relish, because you are doing the right thing by all other students.

You will do more to benefit your class by doing this than on any other day this year.

Letters. Myrna Smith. Spare the rod and spoil the class.

Comment. From about this time in 1975, the States banned the use of the cane in school. The last to do so was Queensland in 1995. But even so, every now and then, the matter raises its head, and depending on the reported state of delinquency in the nation, always finds a number of supporters.

THAT UK REPORT IS JUST ANTI-POM HYPE?

Letters, J Baddock. The front page report of a migrant family returning to Britain for 24 hours, finding it "dead" and yearning for the "not so crowded towns of Australia" must rate as the most fatuous news item of the year.

Imagine a family staying for 24 hours in Sydney on a recent rainy day in the throes of a water, beer and rail strike.

That is enough to make anyone want to migrate to South Vietnam.

And how anyone can see Britain, with its rich and varied cultural life as "dead," a country which is the centre and shrine of most Australians wishing to leave their parochial background, is almost worthy of an item for April Fools' Day - which it wasn't!

Comment. There is something in most Australians that revels in anti-Britain propaganda. If there is a claim that Brits are behaving stupidly, or that their country is falling apart, most Aussies will latch on to it, enjoy talking about it, and savour it. The reason generally is that they know it is an irrelevance, and they know it is wrong. It is all part of a slanging match that both nations engage in. It is part of the easy and special relationship that we have with each other.

If that report was real, then what a family of dills they are. If it is not, then I trust that each of you will take it and exaggerate it and spread the lie with all the frivolity that it deserves.

A SERIOUS ATTACK ON CHRISTIANITY?

Letters, P Jones. I have just received my booklet on Medibank and with it a specimen of the claim form. I am saddened to note that we will be asked to insert our "First given name" and not our Christian name. Have we now abandoned all claim to being a Christian society? Are we ashamed of our faith and our Christian heritage?

I hope that many of us will see fit to amend this and other similar forms and substitute the word "Christian" for "given", thereby openly protesting against this further attempt to impose secular values on our society.

Comment. This type of Letter usually comes with the Christmas season. Then Letters point out that Xmas should really be called Christmas, and warns that Christianity is under attack, and suffering peril.

Comment. It seems to me that Christianity at this moment had more to worry about than that.

Letters, N Khan, I Kleinberg, S Gandhi, A El-Khalidi.

In reply to P Jones, who throws up his hands in holy dismay at Medibank's request for "first given name" rather than "Christian name," we would like to point out that the undersigned have no Christian name to give.

COUNTRY LIVING

Olde Sydney Town is a fake town built out in the bush, about 40 miles north of Sydney. It represents life in a village with shops and bars and a Police Station. It also has convicts, stage coaches and all the junk of the Wild Colonial Days. Women are dressed in gingham, men in fancy overalls, each family carries a mock, but real, shot-gun. It imagines life in a romanticised village, two hundred years ago.

One of the acts performed each day is the flogging of convicts by Policemen. Thirty lashes and a washing down with vinegar. Great viewing, and many visitors loudly chant the count along with the policeman.

But the flogger might get a bit vigorous, and a few prisoners complained. No, says the Landlord, the owner of the business, the flogging is not too hard, and offers to be the victim at the next flogging. Their public argument aroused much interest among the crowd.

So up he fronts, half bare, and receives 40 of the best. And then proclaims that it did not hurt at all.

That seemed to make everyone very happy, including the Police, and the Landlord, and the big crowd that gathered to watch the flogging. Heaps of them mustered at the bar, and fun spilled over until past the closing time.

This spectacle so pleased the crowd that the whole act was now carried over, and became a favoured part of the daily show.

A DIFFERENT POINT OF VIEW

Letters, (Mrs) T Schaer. The actors at Olde Sydney Town who take part in the daily whippings, floggings and beatings are, according to your report in the Herald today, finding it all a bit too realistic for comfort. They will, I am afraid, receive little sympathy from me. The whole sadistic performance should never have been allowed in the first place.

All countries, unfortunately, have in their history periods of violence and brutality. None, to my knowledge, glories in it as Australia does.

The serious student can find in any public library plenty of written descriptions of these unhappy events. The sickening display at

Olde Sydney Town can only appeal to those of perverted tastes and give nightmares to children unfortunate enough to be dragged along to them.

Comment. A lot of people would disagree.

PATIENTS' RIGHTS

Letters. Martin Cusack. Might I respond to Mr Ahlston about the dissatisfied patient who does not want to receive some treatment.

That patient has the right to change doctors at any time. If there is a time limit, then the recalcitrant patient can choose to accept treatment, or perhaps die. He can choose himself. But he does have a choice.

TOUGH RULES FOR A FAMILY

Letters, R Chaunavel. I was under the impression, which appears to be false, that the welfare of the family unit meant a great deal to the present Government.

Three and a half years ago I returned to this country with my daughter to rejoin my husband and eldest son. I left behind my 16-year-old son, who was in London as guitarist in a group. I was content to do this, under the impression he could join us when he was ready.

When I sent his fare in January, I telephoned the Immigration Department to ask if he had to go through any formalities; I was told he couldn't come as he doesn't have a required trade.

My son then applied for a working holiday visa; this was refused. We then signed guarantor forms for him to obtain a holiday visa, which was also refused on the grounds that if he came, he would only want to stay as all his family, including his grandmother, are here. He could not be considered a bona fide tourist.

I pointed out to the Immigration Department that I am, in effect, being denied the right to ever see this child again. As a family we find this situation intolerable. His brother has served this country and fought in Vietnam. In return he is refused the right to have his brother over here.

Is this kind of situation really the intention of the new immigration regulations, or just one of the in-built anomalies?

Comment. On the face of it, it looks like a tough deal for the family. Maybe news will crop up in the next few days that says something will be done about it.

HOT TOPIC

A controversy, over smoking in cabs by cabbies, has erupted. Should these persons be allowed to smoke and drive. There are currently no laws directing cabbies either way.

An *SMH* reporter took a few cab rides to ask the cabbies. One replied to the question "Well they could ping me right now on three counts. Firstly, I have not had a shave. Second, I am smoking without the passenger's permission. Third, I have my arm out the cab,

But what the hell. You've got to be free." Along with other drivers, he said that if a passenger objected, he would throw the cigarette out the window. "No problems."

It seems as though cabbies will soon lose their freedom. Voices are growing to ban the practice, and a magistrate in Brisbane imposed the ban on a cabbie yesterday.

If it is important to you, there is only a little time left. My suggestion is that if you **do** want a cab-ride with a smoking driver, you should book one soon.

WHITLAM'S TURN OF PHRASE

Letters, (Rev) W O'Reilly, President General, Methodist Church of Australasia. No matter how justifiable the anger of the Prime Minister concerning the recent actions of the Queensland Premier, Mr Bjelke-Petersen, there can be no justification for describing him as a "Bible-bashing bastard".

Mr Whitlam would do well to note that there are still millions of Australians who look to their Prime Minister to show more restraint and to refrain from such public indecencies.

JUNE NEWS ITEMS

Medibank will begin operating **for all citizems on July 1st.** Some of the details have been announced, and various parties have considered their response....

700 Doctors had a combined meeting at the week-end and unanimously **agreed to take industrial action** if certain provisions about hospitals were introduced....

Details of the dispute are not needed here. Suffice to note that many of the parties are coming out of the woodwork and reacting unfavourably to some provisions. **This opposition can be expected over the coming months**, so you can bet that the introduction will not be plain sailing.

Lance Barnard, the Federal Minister for Defence, will accept a diplomatic post overseas, effective immediately. This move has the blessing of Gough Whitlam. But is violently opposed by the Federal Treasurer, Dr Jim Cairns, supposedly Whitlam's right-hand man....

Cairns expects that Barnard's departure will result in a by-election for the vacant seat. He fears that it will then be lost to Labor, and the Government's hold on the House of Representatives weakened. ....

June 4. **This could be the straw that breaks the camel's back.** Whitlam and Cairns have been unhappy with each other for months, and it is unlikely that the situation can continue for much longer....

Is Labor in trouble?

Oh dear. Another Whitlam move that will be unpopular with voters. In the 1972 election, he promised that he would **remove the means test on pensioners** aged 65-70. The promised time to do this is now up, but he announced that it would not be included in this year's budget....

This will be unpopular with pensioners and their families. **These are voters with long memories.**

June 7. My guess of three day's ago was correct. Jim Cairns **was** removed as Treasurer, and he was replaced by Bill Hayden. It is generally considered that Hayden will be a lot more conservative than Cairns was. On this news, **the Stock Market rose to a new record.**

A by-election was held for **the electorate of Bass**, to replace Lance Barnard. In what was supposed to be a safe Labor seat, **the Labor candidate was beaten by one of the largest margins ever...**

This **augurs poorly for the Labor Party** at the next Federal election....

Punters are changing the odds for that election. A few months ago, Labor was odds on. Now, **Liberals are light favorites, and gaining quickly.**

THOUGHTS ON INFLATION

Letters, W Gowe, Medical Practitioner. This country is now at the crossroads of decision as regards inflation. If this opportunity is missed, then down the mine we go, the same way as the Brits! The inmates of that little island off the French coast stopped working years ago, but are still clamouring for more dough.

Let's face it, we're only a little way behind. How on earth can people expect the employers to pay more and still not tack on the extra costs to the price of their products? Or do they really think that the companies should be satisfied with little or no profits?

Price indexation appears to be one factor that can help, but it's going to be no more than a help. If we don't all take a personal stand on the issue, then we've got what's coming to us. Remember the Brits!

As a gesture I'm prepared to knock back the increase in medical fees as foreshadowed by the AMA to take effect as from July 1, if others will do the same. If they won't, then that increase won't be worth much anyhow.

Will a few trade unionists join me?

The Letter above is really nothing new. It once again tells the world that the wage-inflation spiral is still in existence, and that general increases in wages are always eaten up by inflation. Workers might get ahead for a month or so, but increased costs soon catch up. **It's an old message**, but one that gets forgotten in the hurly burley of mortgages and rapid inflation.

That is the world right now. Inflation is about 17 per cent, and everyone is claiming for wage increases. On top of that, Government Ministers in most Departments are so anxious to get their pet projects off the ground that they are willing to pay out generously.

Part of the grand battle that took place in the last month involved Whitlam versus Cairns. Whitlam had a fairly careful approach to spending, but his Ministers did not. Cairns, then Treasurer, was most generous in supporting the financing of all sorts of dreams. So a battle raged for months, with dire consequences for Cairns.

In any case, here again is a Letter on the dangers of the wage-inflation spiral. As usual, no one took any notice of those dangers. So those demands, and the concessions to them, continued at a merry pace.

MORE ON JIM CAIRNS

When the axe fell on Cairns. Whitlam executed a re-shuffle of his Cabinet, and changed portfolios to get what he thought would be a better mix of talents.

His first victim was Jim Cairns. He was moved to a position of no significance. A mighty fall, from the exalted position of Treasurer.

The new Treasurer, Les Hayden, made his position clear immediately. He wanted Australia to practice austerity at all levels.

But the Australian Medical Association had just replied to a Wages judgement and rejected the proposed fee increase. They had been offered a four per cent increase, and instead demanded a 12 per cent rise. This suited Hayden quite well, for he was able to speak against the Doctors, but also give the wider community a lesson on the virtues of wage restraint.

His speech received good publicity, and the die was cast. The Treasurer was firmly set of wage and spending restraint, and the spenders in the Government had best play heed.

A DANGER WARNING FROM FRASER

Malcolm Fraser had now been Leader of the Opposition for over a month, and had been pretty quiet. He had voiced a few opinions on the refugee crisis in Vietnam, but stayed well short of anything contentious. Now, he showed the first real sign of taking on Whitlam in direct personal conflict in Parliament.

This was a matter about whether Whitlam had lied to Parliament. It was obvious that he had not, but Fraser moved for a censure motion any way.

There was no doubt that the motion would fail. In fact it was 69 to 62. It was just a symbolic statement to Fraser. It said to Whitlam that Malcolm Fraser is ready for battle, and that he is out to get you. Get ready for a real battle this time.

From this time onwards, Fraser kept his promise. He harassed and blocked Whitlam at every possible chance. For the next six months, Fraser became more and more confrontational to Whitlam, blocking his every move, and knocking back much of the legislation proposed for the Senate.

HOUSEWIVES' PERPETUAL LAMENT

Letters, M McMahon. During the school holidays, I endeavoured to purchase a reasonably priced school jumper for my son. I went to three different stores and found that the prices varied from $12 (locally for the school's own jumper) to $17.50 for a plain grey school jumper, without the school's colours.

While I appreciate that there have been many price increases, I fail to understand how manufacturers and retail stores can charge so much for a commodity which is purchased by so many people. For every size of jumper, there must be at least several hundred purchasers and I feel the costs could therefore be reduced. The stores would certainly not sell several hundred ordinary jumpers, which are usually priced at about $8 to $10. In fact, I did purchase a plain grey jumper for $8 which will just have to suffice for my son.

As he is only 14 and is in 3rd form, he could still be growing and it could be necessary for me to purchase more than one uniform in a year.

I think it's about time the manufacturers thought about the homemaker in this International Women's Year, and brought down the prices for school items to a reasonable level. They must make a tremendous profit, as school principals are, as a rule, strict as far as pupils wearing school uniform are concerned.

Comment. The mother in the home usually makes a big contribution to the Letters pages of newspapers. Most of their Letters are complaints about inequities handed out to them. And the one topic that comes up most is the cost of school clothing.

Another subject that often appears is the high price of imported family goods. It might be fly spray, hair rollers, carpet, or clothing and shoes. Writers say that the price of these is double the prices in England or America or Japan. Given, of course, the appropriate currency conversion. Every one of these writers include somewhere in their Letter a direct accusation that someone somewhere is running a racket, and has a well-worked out operation to do this.

Comment. They are probably right. I can say that over the 37 years that I have covered in writing these books, this same charge has been levelled year after year. Could so many mothers possibly be wrong?

REMEMBER PHONEY NAMES?

Most readers will remember the old phone books, called Directories. In Sydney, for example, there was a White Pages, two Volumes each of about 1,000 pages to serve as a directory that allowed callers to look up the numbers of registered phone renters.

Then there was a Pink Pages, that gave the numbers of Businesses. Followed by the Yellow pages.

Every one with a phone took these books for granted. If you had a phone connected, you had them delivered to your home about once a year. And every city and country town had its own books.

The collation of these books was a huge task. So too was the printing and distribution of them to most households in the nation. Collectively, they made a big industry.

Well, now they are mainly gone. Some cities scratch out a few *Guides to Businesses* by the local Chamber of Commence. And of course, the Internet provides all sort of alternatives.

Comment. If you are lucky enough to still have a copy of a White Pages Directory, I invite you to examine it and see it as a bit of a wonder. After all, it is a document, issued to every household in the nation, immense in its scope, carefully spell-checked, carrying the name of most families in the nation. It is a wonderful feat.

And of course, it's second purpose is also bountiful. In the large areas that did not have access to toilet paper, especially in country regions, the old Directories were always welcome as a substitute in the dunny. As one reader expressed it, "In the end, I prefer the phone books, because they have a much better finish than newspapers."

WATER PROBLEMS

In 1975, most of the country was not sewered. Cities had some coverage, radiating out from the sewage treatments works. The service spread only so far, and this was becoming an increasingly popular demand.

But large numbers in the country regions had no town water in their homes. Most of these had water tanks or pumped water from dams. Some country people carried water from town in their lorries, a daily load at a time. So this lack of town water too was a problem But even those householders, who had the luxury of both sewer and town water, still had their woes.

Letters, A Houston. The most equitable method of assessing contributions to municipal councils and the Water Board, and at the same time reducing the volume of work of the Valuer-General's Department, is simple.

As municipal council services (administration, health, roads, lighting, etc) are equally available to the benefit of all residents of the municipality, and bear no relation whatever to land size or value, a poll tax on all residents 18 years and over, assessed to cover council's estimated yearly expenditure, is surely equitable.

The Water Board should charge on usage. In many dwellings there are three or fewer residents, while in other dwellings (in close proximity, used as rooming houses) there are possibly up to 10 residents. It is very obvious that the quantity of water used in the second type of dwelling would be much greater than that used in the first. It is possible, and indeed probable, that the water rates for the dwelling with two occupants are much greater than the dwelling with many more occupants.

At a meeting at Neutral Bay two years ago, a spokesman for the Water Board said that it would be impossible to read the water meters, but if the various gas companies and electricity bodies can read their meters quarterly **why can't the Water Board meter readers do so annually?** I understand the board insists on installation of a meter whenever there is a change of owner.

Municipal and Water Board rates are the only two services arbitrarily determined.

Letters, D Culpin. Why should the charge for water, sewerage and drainage services be complicated by wealth distribution considerations? Surely, as with the charges for electricity, gas, the telephone, etc, the user of water, sewerage and drainage services should be charged only the cost of providing them.

This cost depends mainly on the area of the block of land serviced, the length of its street frontage, and certain characteristics of the surrounding terrain. Any relationship between the cost of the service and the market value of the land is purely fortuitous. An approximate formula for the cost, based on two or three characteristics of the land serviced, could be readily devised.

The fact that the owner of a more valuable block of land may have the capacity to pay higher charges is as irrelevant to what he should be charged for water as it is to what he should be charged for electricity. For the same service, everyone should pay the same charge. It is in the sphere of taxation that wealth-income redistribution measures should be located, not in providing services.

Letters, B Zecchin. In regard to Water Board accounts, your correspondent, J H Doyle, should consider himself extremely lucky only having an excess charge of $50.60 on his rates for March, 1973 to March, 1975.

I am a widow and also an invalid pensioner, occupying my home alone, except for one young lodger, and my excess charges for this period are $116. I also have only one bathroom, and few requirements for water use.

Plumbing charges of $63 to try and trace a possible leak, plus $5 to check the meter, combine with the excess water charge to make this an impossible amount to meet. I receive only the usual $62 per fortnight and am allowed to earn only a very small amount under the social security rules.

Letters, M Vaile. I was staggered to learn of the admission to the Australian Journalists' Association of seven new members - all photographers for the Metropolitan Water Board.

SEVEN photographers for the MWS and DB? No wonder we are about to be doused with water rate increases ranging from 36 per cent.

Comment. I am reminded by the Letters above of living my childhood in a small mining town in the Cessnock coalfields. This town of 2,000 people was cut in halves by a railway track for carrying coal.

Town water was new to the area, so about half the town had water, and the other half did not. My family did, but the next-door neighbour did not. I remember that, in severe droughts, when the tanks had gone dry, each afternoon at sunset one of the children from next door, would come to our back door and ask "Could I please get a bucket of water." For a family with five girls, this was a tough time indeed. Incidentally, the half town on the other side of he railway line did not get town water for another ten years.

JULY NEWS ITEMS

In a spectacular manner, Gough Whitlam had removed the commission of his Deputy, Jim Cairns. **Cairns has now been sacked from the Cabinet....**

The two most powerful politicians in the nation fell out over some correspondence that Whitlam judged to have emanated from Cairns. Cairns denied this to Parliament. Whitlam apparently did not believe him and said he had misled Parliament. **Thus Cairns had to go. He left truculently....**

This sensation of a major split in the senior ranks of the Labor Party occurred within a week of a major loss in a by-election in Bass, Tasmania. There were thus many **calls for Fraser to push for an early election**. But he chose not to do so.

The Labor Party has what is called a Caucus. It consists of all elected Federal Members, both Senate and House. It is this body that appoints every minister including the Prime Minister....

In a special meeting on July 15, it decided to **endorse the sacking of Jim Cairns**. But this meeting also issued many warnings that **Labor was on thin ice electorally**, and could afford no more controversies.

Football fans of all Codes are familiar with **large numbers of children running on to the field** at the end of a game....

After a dangerous incident last week, moves are afoot to **ban the practice** for Rugby League, with no doubt that it will spread to all sports. And indeed it did, sensibly I suppose. Pity though.

It was a **sad day for the family of Jim Cairns** yesterday. One of their pet cats was hit on the road by a car, and died as a result....

Mrs Cairns said "Jimmy just phoned me from Canberra, and I had to tell him. **We both cried.**"

The **President of the ACTU, Bob Hawke**, was looming as a prospective politician. He **had the support of most of the Labour movement....**

It was suggested by many that he might enter politics, and indeed, replace Gough Whitlam as the Prime Minister. He was a Rhodes Scholar, and was very popular with rank-and-file unionists. **The next step in his career should be into politics....**

He was famous for the fact that **he liked a beer or two after work**, and it was sometimes said that this could be a disadvantage if he went into politics....

At a Press conference, **he reassured the public** that if he got elected he would give up drinking completely. Some reported that **they thought this impossible....**

They were right.

HALF-TIME REPORT

With the year half gone, a summary of how Labor is going is appropriate. As I look back over the last six months, I see a procession of events that **together paint a dismal picture for Labor**. Against a background of high unemployment continuing and high interest rates, there **must** be a drop in Labor's popularity.

Superimposed on this month after month, with no relief in sight, **the various battles within the Party** gave the impression that the Party was dominated by Whitlam himself, and that it was in disarray.

The *SMH* had a similar opinion in its Editorial. It ran a headline "Gough's Going Great" and it explained that this was a slogan used by Labor at the national election a year ago. But now it had the "Great" omitted, so that it read simply "Gough's Going."

It went on to say "Rarely in Australian politics had a reputation dwindled so quickly." "The man has been "unteachable". And the harshest words of all. "His style of government has continued as it began, wedded in its own kind of remote, inflexible paternalism, governing wilfully, unpredictably and worryingly."

Comment. I suspect that if an election were held right now for the House, Whitlam and the Libs would be about equal.

RAISING LOANS IN AUSTRALIA

There are lots of reasons why Australia needs to borrow big money from overseas. We, as a small nation, with a huge territory, need money to develop the cities and infrastructure and industries to the point of self-sufficiency. This so far has taken over 200 years, and the rate of borrowing shows no sign of slowing down.

But, more immediately, we need more money to repay previous loans, and more money to buy fleets of aircraft and to buy battle ships. No one should imagine that such sums can be financed by taking it out of annual Budgets. **We would never get anything done if we waited for budgets big enough to do this.** So, we borrow, and repay on a regular basis.

As a nation, we do this through recognised markets in London, New York, Japan and Switzerland. If the likely borrower is a Government Department, then it needs to get Parliamentary approval and then **leave it to the Treasury to arrange the loan**. If they are private corporations, such as Qantas wanting to borrow for a fleet of aircraft, they must use virtually the same process. That is, get Treasury permission and leave it to them to settle the loan.

Right now, several Ministers in the Whitlam Government had **big spending ideas. Rex Connor** was one of these. He was the Minister for Minerals and Energy. He had ambitious plans to develop the nation.

He saw, correctly, that mining and export of minerals was done on an amateurish basis, and that the small -scale existing mining industry could be developed into a major world player. Among his plans to fix this was a scheme to borrow cash from an overseas source and, for example, develop a grid that would carry oil from the oil-fields to all parts of Australia.

Such plans required much money. And there were quite a few Ministers who had their own ambitious plans. So the ideas developed among the more renegade Ministers that such borrowings could be arranged somehow by using brokers outside the normal Treasury route. That is, in particular, via Arab sources, who were now rich with money from the high price of oil at the time.

In late 1974, and early 1975, Cabinet was persuaded to grant permission to allow Connor to begin negotiations with an Arab, called Kemlani, concerning a loan for the huge sum of four Billion dollars.

Mr Kemlani and his team visited Australia, and it became apparent that they were not like most brokers, but were seen by some to fit the description of gangsters rather than brokers.

So that, at the end of June, nothing definite had been arranged. But Connor's zeal was still strong, and equally strong was Treasury's resolve that **it** should not be left out of the process.

Over the next six months, this situation will develop rapidly, and will become known as the Kemlani Affair. Eventually it will discredit the whole Government and make it the subject of much ridicule.

We will follow this Affair, with many of its sub-plots, as it develops.

FRASER'S FIRST FAILURE

Malcolm Fraser had only been Leader of the Opposition for a few months, and had trod cautiously. But things were moving too quickly and he just **had** to throw his hat into the ring.

The cause for excitement was the Loans Affair. The various Ministers thought they could evade Treasury supervision and control, and borrow huge sums of money directly from international sources. So by now, our capital markets in the big cities, and Canberra, were full of slick money brokers who were talking big money, and it was suggested that not only would they get high interest rates for their cash, but also large sums for broking a deal. The sharks were really barking, if I can mangle the language.

All of these agents had publicity machines with them, so the cities were full of success stories about progress towards fixing a loan or two. Equally, there were denials, or suggestions of successes. Kemlani featured in all this excitement, but there were many others getting into the act.

But it was hard to put a finger on any misdoings in the ranks of the Government handling these offerings. So now Fraser acted. He gambled that if he held an enquiry into the activity, he could find some Public Servants who were hopefully helping themselves to the potential rivers of gold. So he arranged a Senate Enquiry into the activity for mid-July.

A Senate Enquiry is a big event. It is like a Royal Commission, without some of its powers, where its decisions had the capacity to destroy careers and causes at its will. What Fraser intended to do was to quiz a dozen Departmental Heads, and hope to get evidence to embarrass the Labor Government.

For the next ten days, Canberra was in turmoil. Whitlam and dozens of sitting Members and past Members, said that this was not legal. Or that it was legal. Or that it was interfering with the present and future Separation of the Powers. Or that it was, or was not, either this or that.

On the day of the hearing, the twelve executives were told by the Government that they were not to answer any questions, **that they had been gagged**. After that, and a few days of confusion, the hearing collapsed, and Mr Fraser's bid for clarification failed.

That was not good for Fraser's image. It was even worse for Whitlam. Accusations were raised, and heeded by most Australians, that the gagging of Australia's top Public Servants, had been done to protect the Government from the exposure of unfavourable secrets.

As it turned out, there were no such secrets, but who was to know that at the time. **The clear implication was that the Labor Government had something to hide**, and so their slide in popularity continued.

DANGEROUS DRIVING

The road toll was too high, and every State reported the same thing. And they all reported that it was on the increase. Comments on this were plentiful.

Letters, G Ramsay. I consider that an ordinary class 1 licence should only permit a person to drive a car up to a maximum power rating. Should a person wish to drive a more powerful car than this, he or she should be required to pass a demanding advanced driving test.

Insurance companies impose heavy premiums on drivers under 25 for very sound reasons and, in proposing this, I am thinking mainly of inexperienced youngsters who thrash around in extremely powerful vehicles capable of speeds well over 100 mph. I would feel much happier on the open roads if transport drivers were required to pass this advanced test also.

Regarding the speed limit, I think we should turn to New Zealand's experience of imposing a national maximum limit of 50 mph. It is common knowledge that this limit was set to save fuel during the energy crisis, and the remarkable drop in road casualties which resulted was not expected. That energy crisis has passed but the speed limit of 50 mph remains. Maybe we should give this more thought.

Road discipline in this country, is almost non-existent by Western standards. I think we should make a greater effort to educate our drivers and what better way than through the medium of TV. We all hear, or used to, that "smoking is a health hazard." Surely bad driving is more of a hazard. An intelligent approach to this on TV, possibly using animated material, would be welcome and could only do good.

Letters, (Dr) B Pollard. You regularly publish the progressive totals of road deaths for the year in this State - on June 28, it was 641. I wish to make several points.

Appalling though this figure is, it goes nowhere near the real extent of the tragedy. As a doctor who spends most of his working life in an operating theatre, I have been involved virtually every week for more than 20 years with the attempted restoration of those who are not killed - at least, not outright - in road accidents. Very often, it seems the victim would have been better off to have been killed.

We know that approximately 80 per cent of these accidents are associated with high blood-alcohol levels, whether in car occupants or pedestrians.

I realise that strong emotions are generated when desperate measures are proposed to deal with desperate situations, and when the remedy infringes civil liberties. But I would like to make a strong recommendation for everyone, including the government, to consider. I do so chiefly on behalf of the innocents, either dead, maimed, or bereft of those on whom they depended for love or support.

I suggest that a vigorous campaign of instruction be commenced in order to warn everybody of coming consequences, and this to last, say, three months. After this time, all drivers found with a blood-alcohol level higher than that permitted by law, whether in an accident or not, would **be deprived of their licence for 10 years**, without any exception or redress whatever. If the offence was repeated during the suspension, a heavy jail sentence would automatically follow.

I believe lesser measures have failed.

Letters, M F Dixon. I believe that if legislation was passed compelling every driver convicted of causing a serious road accident, or of driving at a speed dangerous to the public, to **fit a governor** to his car limiting its speed to 50 mph for a period fixed by the court, we should have 50 per cent less accidents within a matter of weeks.

THE LOANS AFFAIR

Australians everywhere were becoming alarmed by the sums of money being sought as loans, by all sorts of Federal Ministers. **Even the Prime Minister** was anxious to get enough to finance **his** grand plan for a single Railway adventure that would link the nation.

The first thing on everyone's mind was who would pay it back? How would it be financed? After that, there was a multitude of Letters that either blamed the Government for its folly, or perhaps praised it for its courage and breaking with Treasury tradition.

Letters, S Heatley. The longer the controversy over the Federal Government's approach to raising overseas loans dags on, the more the trend of events can be likened to those of the Watergate affair - the denials of complicity, the gradual forced disclosures and the continuous implication of public figures.

Do these events portend the gravest culmination here, as in the US, which resulted in the disgrace and resignation of President Richard Nixon?

Letters, (Mrs) M Graham. In reply to your editorials etc, on the Labor Government, on Mr Whitlam, PM, and his Deputy.

Will you please tell me and other readers what crimes they have committed, as they have not borrowed one petro-dollar, or paid out one Australian dollar in commission.

The free world has no dollars to lend, so why should not our Government borrow petro-dollars if it can? Remember, it was the free world's dollar, know-how, and expert men that first made the petro-dollar available to the Arabs or Middle East.

Letters, W Harrison. I was astounded at the Prime Minister's ill-advised pun last Wednesday on the RSL's Ode of Remembrance.

Speaking in the loans debate, he is reported to have facetiously quipped "The Age will not **query** them, it will just condemn."

The accepted words are, of course, "Age shall not **weary** them nor the years condemn."

The ode as a whole is an acknowledgment of our debt to the dead of four wars and it has been, and will continue to be, recited at thousands of gravesides throughout Australia and overseas.

I was astounded also at the raucous laughter with which the Prime Minister's colleagues greeted this scintillating piece of wit.

Despite their brashness, these people in Canberra must surely realise that some things are sacred.

An apology would be appropriate.

Letters, J Godfrey. Because no money has apparently changed hands, there appears to be no question of impropriety by the Australian Government in its loan-raising activities. This is not the point at issue.

What worries me so greatly, and no doubt many others, is the **appalling naivete, credulousness and incompetence displayed by our elected leaders in this field**. Have they considered the effect on Australia of the influx of such huge sums? Have they any concrete ideas of how they intend to spend it, and whether these projects, whatever they may be, will be sufficiently viable to enable the interest to be paid, let alone the capital repaid? If not, how is it intended such payments will be made? What will be the effects on our currency, overseas balances and inflationary pressures?

Letters, (Mrs) R Hails. I would like to support the letters of M Graham and F Imber.

Just what crimes have been committed? Is it wrong for Mr Whitlam to want to buy Australia back? It should never have been sold in the first place by the previous Government.

His desires have always been clear to me: To give people their rights, so long denied them, and to do all he could to strengthen and aid the family unit wherever poverty and its accompanying miseries threatened to destroy it.

He has done magnificently since he was elected in 1972 in spite of the unremitting pressure of powerful groups. So much unemployment would not have existed and inflation have been decreased had he been allowed to govern.

Letters, F Imber. Any letter "knocking" the Whitlam Government seems assured of space in your columns. Especially whining observations like those of M Allen about Mr Whitlam's failure to abolish the means test for pensioners in the 65 years' group.

Well, I have been retired less than two years and since then the combined pension cheque for wife and husband has increased from $75 to $120 - a rise of 60 per cent. The means test has been abolished for two age groups. The third has been deferred; so what!

The jackals are gathering for the kill now, but God help pensioners when the Liberal-Country Party takes power as seems likely with the aid of a powerful and biased press.

Comment. The above Letters show about an equal number for and against. That was just to show you the range of ideas. **But in fact, the number opposed to the borrowing was the much greater.**

AUGUST NEWS ITEMS

Juni Morosi, formally the principal private secretary to ex-Treasurer, **Dr Jim Cairns**, announced that **she is pregnant**. Asked for comment, Cairns said that every child is welcome, provided it has a parent who loves it.

Let us all hope that the pregnancy and birth goes without a hitch.

Patrick Partners, **a well-to-do Sydney stock trading corporation, has gone into receivership**. The failure of this company to meet its obligations is **sending a shiver though investors and brokers** throughout the nation.

In NSW, **the number of children waiting for adoption had dropped** substantially. As a consequence, persons over 38 will no longer be considered as adopters....

Many would-be parents, aged over 38, are quite upset at this, and claim they have waited in a queue for years, just to be disappointed as they were right now

Caucus announced that all **Ministers and senior Public Servants must in future fly in economy class**, instead of at any higher rate available....

Looks like tomorrow's Budget will be tough, if the **Canberra lot are cutting down on their perks**....

In fact, the Budget was OK. It was balanced, everyone got a bit, and everyone lost a bit. It was a hold-the-fort effort.....

Many people wanted it to be harsh, with austerity, supposedly to counter inflation. **Others wanted it to be expansionary** to get the badly lagging economy moving again. ...

And Ministers, and their acolytes, **hoped to get packets of money** that would finance their hair-brained day-dreaming. Instead, it was a document that sensibly balanced the huge complexity of competing pressures....

But, like all Governments before them, **the excise on beer, tobacco, and petrol was increased**, enough to hurt.

In England, the Third and **final Cricket Test** was heading for a result that would have decided who kept the Ashes for the next few years....

After two days play, marauders raided the pitch at night, **drilled holes in the turf, and filled them with oil.** This seeped, and made the pitch unplayable....

The match was declared a draw, and this meant that the Series went to Australia. And that Australia kept the Ashes....

When will the Poms capitulate once and for all? Pouring oil on the pitch is the last resort.

ROOS FOR THE TABLE?

A scientist from the Federal Department of the Environment suggested that canned Kangaroo meat would be good for consumers, and the national income.

An official from the Kangaroo Protection Committee had something to say about this.

Letters, M Wilson, Kangaroo Protection Committee, Sydney. The only way the NSW Department of Health might reverse its policy, and allow kangaroo meat to be used for human consumption, would be if kangaroos were slaughtered hygienically in supervised abattoirs. To herd kangaroos into abattoirs would subject them to a great deal of stress and this Committee would vigorously fight this cruel method.

It would be far better for the Australian Government to seek **markets for its sheep**, which are domesticated and bred for this purpose, as they must know how much money has already been wasted on futile farming experiments to use kangaroo meat for human consumption. It would be far better also for Mr Wilson of the Federal Department of the Environment to concentrate on other aspects of wildlife conservation, such as seeing that kangaroos are humanely destroyed when blinded by sandflies in hot weather after floods, instead of trying to push the point that Australians want to eat their national heritage.

There is plenty of beef and lamb in Australia for home consumption and overseas, without having to resort to using kangaroo meat.

Letters, W Wilkie. The controversy about eating kangaroos is still running hot, as I note from M Wilson's letter.

It would seem to me to be a storm in a teacup, as anyone who has had anything to do with kangaroos in the wild would know that they are one of the most wormy, maggot-ridden creatures in Australia. The only roos and wallabies that would make it past a preliminary inspection at a competent meatworks would be those in the zoos around Australia, and there are not enough there to make a decent bowl of soup.

May I suggest to those people who want to eat kangaroos that they switch their attention to snakes. The fillets are of convenient size, easy to cook, and eating snakes would reduce the danger to the human population.

Letters, E Sobiesiak. W Wilkie does not know as much about kangaroos and the edibility of their flesh as he supposes.

Kangaroos in some regions of Australia will have worm-infested flesh, but once cooked the meat is quite safe to eat. A young kangaroo from the highland areas is a very healthy animal, free from domestic stock diseases and maladies, and is as palatable as any lamb or bullock.

I am sure that the only maggot-ridden kangaroo W Wilkie has seen (if he has seen any at all) is a fly-blown dead one, not sought after as food except by scavengers.

To admit that zoos are the only places where healthy kangaroos thrive is not only a fallacy but a farce, and I am glad I live where I do.

Comment. As most people have found out since, the taste of well-prepared roo meat is about as good as meat from cattle and sheep. From a marketing point of view, the supply of snakes is not large enough to justify marketing them.

In any case, imagine the complaints from the Snake Protection Society.

Second comment. My Editor tells me that roo has a gamey taste, and is robust like streak. She adds that snake is sweet, like rabbit, but that it makes you hiss at night.

REMEMBER CHILD ENDOWMENT?

Child endowment,as such, by the 2020's has disappeared altogether It has been replaced and extended by **many schemes to help the family. But in the 1970's it was a big factor in keeping families solvent.** It was a regular fortnightly payment, by the Government, of a sum of money to each family that had children. It varied from time to time and place to place, but it was large enough to be significant. I can remember as a child, the weekly payment was five Shillings, but only for the first child.

Many housewives could not pay the butcher's bill until they went each fortnight to the Post Office to collect their endowment payment. Standover men from local bookies saved their visits to delinquent punters until after Endowment day. It was a regular payment that came in, regardless of strikes and unemployment. For decades, including 1975, it was part and parcel of balancing the budget of most families in the nation.

Any variation in it was a matter of concern, given the current expectation that any change is always for the worse. **The writer below expresses the uncertainties that many people felt.**

Letters, (Mrs) C Boir. As Mr Hayden is preparing the August Budget, I hope he is giving the matter of child endowment some attention.

Since the Budget of 1971, there has been no increase in child endowment. A typical family like ours with children in their teens now costs twice as much to feed and three times as much to clothe and educate than in 1971.

If somebody had proposed in 1971 to reduce child endowment by 50 per cent over a period of four years, there would have been an uproar. And yet, this is exactly what has happened.

It can be argued that this particular benefit is unnecessary. Middle-class families are smaller now and do not need it and working-class people could well be encouraged to have bigger families when endowment would be increased - something we do not want either.

I would therefore like to ask when and why was child endowment introduced? Is it a democratic right or is it a handout, the magnitude of which depends on the mood of the benefactor? Why does the Government shower us with many generous and sometimes unasked for gifts and, at the same time, neglect to fulfil existing obligations? Much as I dislike to suggest this, is it because children do not vote?

I believe Mr Hayden to be a sincere man, who is concerned with the welfare of people. He must know that there is still a need for child endowment especially for those families caught up in the misery of unemployment and the rural depression. Increases in this benefit was one of the recommendations of the Henderson Report on Poverty.

Child endowment could be means-tested and an inquiry could be made as to its necessity. **The policy so far gives one the impression child endowment benefit is being phased-out through the back door.**

GO HOME, IF YOU CAN

Every year in writing these books, the same complaints emerge that there are too few houses for the population, that certain needs are not met, and large numbers of people will never own their own home.

Letters, C Moore, Aust Council of Social Service. It is of concern that in the present climate of threats by the Government to limit expenditure, basic housing needs may not be met in the 1975/76 Budget.

To date, housing has been given a very low priority in Budget allocations, and in 1974/75 constituted only 2 per cent of the total Budget.

Public housing is the only opportunity that many low-income earners have to gain access to adequate housing. Throughout Australia, it has been estimated that at least 90,000 people are on the waiting lists for public housing. The waiting period in most cases is intolerable. In New South Wales and South Australia, for example, the average waiting period for a house is four years. Low-interest finance should be allocated to community groups so that they can establish cost-rent co-operatives. Cost-rent co-operatives will offer low-income earners housing in areas near their jobs, at rents they can afford.

Such finance would also allow special-need groups on low incomes to provide housing for members - for example, ethnic groups for recently arrived migrants, the aged, handicapped, single parents, etc. Cost-rent co-operatives also give members an opportunity to participate in housing management.

It is of concern also that the experimental program for homeless persons be expanded and developed. The publicity given to the women's refuges demonstrates the almost untouched demand for such services.

Comment. This Letter could have been written in 1995, in 2115, in 2025. Maybe we should take a serious look at this fact, and get ahead of the persistent backlog in housing.

WOMEN JPs AT RISK

Letters, W Gray, Chairman, JP Tutorial Service. The Senior Coroner's warning to women living alone to be cautious in admitting strangers to their premises is most timely.

Of special significance is the position of **women Justices of the Peace**, who are often single or widowed and live alone.

Many have the mistaken belief that they are bound by duty to service documents at any time and at the client's convenience; this places them at risk and **is quite unnecessary**.

The JP Tutorial Service in its State-wide classes seeks to clarify the many misunderstandings concerning the administration of JP duties, one of the most important being that, as Justices tender an honorary professional service, they **should only grant interviews by appointment at times and places suitable to them**.

There is no need whatever to suffer an invasion of personal privacy; the Commission of the Peace does not require it and rarely would circumstances justify it.

Comment. Sadly, this applies equally well to men JP's in the rougher world of the 2020s.

MEDIBANK INTRODUCTION

The introduction of this vast scheme went quite well. It involved the mailout of one card per family to all parts of Australia in a timely manner. Setting up physical places to do transactions, all the paperwork involved, the staffing of the whole show, and the provisions for the flow of money and information.

If there **were** some shortfalls, it is a wonder there were not a lot more.

The more significant complaints came not from customers, but from various levels of the professions.

Not just from doctors and pharmacists and the legion of others, but also from behind the scenes.

Letters, (Dr) D Rothery. More than a month ago in a letter to the Herald, I asked State and Federal health authorities to state publicly the conditions of work and remuneration for surgeons under Medibank in hospitals.

The State Minister for Health after reviewing overseas health schemes recently made some interesting statements but we have not heard any comments or facts from Federal health authorities - why?

Must we presume, at this late stage, that their reluctance to comment (not abuse) indicates that they do not consider experience, skill and responsibility for operations important or necessary - whether you have cancer or need a heart operation or anything else.

Surgeons feel that continuous hospital/ patient care cannot exist under the proposed intermittent sessional system. No one could adequately look after a seriously ill patient when they have been contracted to attend a hospital perhaps two or four times a week. Politicians apparently can't see this.

Surgeons are the only people who operate on patients and care for them - not politicians - and surely they should know.

Politicians are concerned with the expenses - not patients.

Let's have some facts and not stupid abuse before it is too late.

DRUGS IN SCHOOL

Drugs in schools were a growing problem. Not the killer drugs that abound in the year 2025, but relatively soft drugs, like marihuana.

Letters, (Dr) D Bass. The headlines of The Sydney Morning Herald do not surprise me. The stresses imposed upon children are so great that the only relief from pressure many can find is to take drugs.

As a mother of four and a general practitioner, I am aware of the enormous demands on time and energy that are expected of pupils pursuing academic goals to the exclusion of any relaxation.

The demands start in primary school and increase the older the children become. With the abolition of the examination system, the pressure is unremitting, as every piece of work counts towards the final assessment. No person can continue to function efficiently under continuous pressure, and neither can our children.

An increasing number of children are either brought for consultation or come themselves with symptoms of stress. When their daily timetable is perused, one finds many working a 16 to 18-hour day which includes travelling.

City and country pupils also suffer from long journeys to and from school, as well as the insatiable demand from innumerable teachers of having to write well-informed essays.

When the adult world demands shorter working hours and more leisure, our children can be entitled to feel their work load is unjust. They are losing their joy of learning and, not being able to alter the system, may find relief from the pressure by taking drugs or alcohol.

Letters, J Bowden. I read with concern the article on the drug situation in High schools. My older children encountered drugs in High school five years ago. Now I have a 13-year-old whom I must expose to the same situation.

It seems a classic Catch-22 position. If I keep her away from school, I can be prosecuted and, presumably, if I expose her to **the moral danger in the schools** I should also be liable to prosecution. Which of these two evils should I choose?

Would a moratorium placed on High school attendance for three months or so give a breathing space in which some positive thinking and concerned action could be developed to create schools in which environment and rationale are conducive to the proper welfare of my child?

Comment. Imagine how these mothers would have responded if confronted by the mayhem that faces youngsters today, in 2025.

PRIVET PROGRESS

About a dozen years ago, I published a Title in this Series that talked about the menace that privet presented to the population. At the end, I was quite happy about the progress being made by Councils in scouring this menace,

Letters, T Vesta. If we keep chipping at the concrete of fuddy-duddy Council minds, we may some day break through, making them realise what their apathy is doing to the State, which is being inundated by noxious weeds, mainly privet.

And perhaps they will get their priorities straight, and ban the menace. By then, of course, privet will be overwhelming hundreds of acres, and the cost of eradication will be astronomical.

Poor fella, my country. So mismanaged in almost every field of administration. Grateful thanks to you, Lane Cove Council, for being so forward-looking and wide-awake. May it rub off on to other Councils.

Comment. Mr Vesta's Letter leaves me uneasy. From it, privet is still a menace, I glean that only a few Councils are trying seriously to get rid of it

And generally that the situation has not improved much at all.

SEPTEMBER NEWS ITEMS

Five small children were drowned when a car they were playing in, rolled into an icy river outside Canberra. The location was at a popular holiday spot, and the parents had left them to frolic in the car.

Nine per cent of Senior school children in NSW claim to get **very drunk at least once a month**. Two per cent claim to pass out....

This is from a survey conducted by the Health Commission and the Department of Education.

Comment. Respondents were boys and girls. Maybe the figures are exaggerated by **their characteristic bravado.**

In a recent poll held by the *SMH*, **only 36 per cent said that they would vote for Labor**. This compares with 9 per cent a year ago. ...

Increasing numbers of Liberals in Federal Parliament are advocating that they somehow **force Labor to call an early election**....

How to do this is a question that is being asked more frequently.

The Federal Minister for Aborigines is calling for a Royal Commission into **relations between Police and Aborigines in camps**....

A letter signed by 36 lawyers talks about relations as **appalling, and tells of bashings** in police round -ups as hotels close....

"The odious traditions of bored and lonely country police going round to **the Reserves and stirring up the boongs** unfortunately seem not to be dead."

Nine months after Cyclone Tracey, the Darwin Reconstruction Committee is about to be replaced after it was revealed that **not one house has been built in that time**.

In July, **unemployment rose** by 12,000 to 130,000. This is five per cent of the workforce, and is a **post-war record for the second month in a row**.

Up until now, passenger trains to the country have had **a last carriage that each carried a Travelling Post Offices (TPO)**. In these venerable old carriages, staff worked to sort and bag mail, and drop it off at country railway stations as they passed through....

This service will now cease. It has been used in NSW since 1870. 108 mail officers will be affected, and sent to new positions.

The NSW Bread Act **bans bread baking for hamburgers on a Sunday**. Thus when a baker in Woolongong (NSW) started to sell these, he was charged by the Police. In protest, he gifted 1,000 loaves of bread to the public. **They were legally baked on a Sunday.**

TAKING STOCK

I happen to know that political life in this fair nation will become quite complicated in the next four months, so **it is appropriate to take stock right now**.

Control of the Lower House is with Labor. Control of the Senate rests with the Liberals. That means that the Libs can block any budget items that the Government proposes. That is what has been happening for a few months, so there is a pile up of matters sitting round waiting for something to change. The Ministers proposing them might think they are urgent, but few of them really are.

But one of them is special, and when it becomes urgent, it will be absolutely critical. This is the proposal for the nation's Budget. If this Supply of money is not available to pay the Government's committments, then everyone in the nation will be in deep trouble. No one knows just how deep this will be, but everyone agrees that it must be avoided at all costs it the nation wants to continue as is.

This brings us back to the refusal of the Senate to pass some legislation. At the moment, the Senate is shaping to refuse to Supply the money for the budget. There us a deadline on this. Get the money by the end of November, or the Government will default, and all hell will be here.

So, this is the threat that is developing. Fraser and the Liberals thinks that if an election were held today, the Liberals would win easily. So too does Labor. But Malcolm Fraser, leader of the Liberals, is not certain, so he is holding his hand for the present. Despite the pressure on him from within his Party, be is not yet rcady to refuse Supply.

But there is another side to this. An election involving both Houses of Parliament cannot just be called by anyone, say the Prime Minister. **It must be approved by the Governor General. And he must have a very good reason to do so.**

At the moment, Labor appears unpopular, but looks can be deceiving. And can change in a day or so. If Whitlam, or Fraser, called for a Double Dissolution right now, the GG would refuse and say that there is nothing really serious currently threatening good government. **So, in reality, right now, forget all the talk about such an event.**

But keep in mind, among all the machinations going on, that the prospect is looming just over the horizon. If circumstances change, and the GG sees that the government is in danger of defaulting on Supply, or of not being able to govern, then a Double Dissolution will be a likely event.

Until that happens, it is government as usual. Labor is hoping for a miracle. Maybe interest rates will fall, or maybe unemployment will drop. Then Labor will regain popularity, and have no fears.

On the other hand, the Liberals are also waiting for a miracle. Maybe one of Whitlam's Ministers will really blow it, or Fraser might somehow change into a popular matinee idol. Then, goodo, bring on the election.

One thing is certain. The chaos around Parliament is leaving it unworkable. Something has to give.

DON'T RUBBISH AUSTRALIA

Many writers complain that we citizens drop our rubbish all over the place, and make no effort to keep the streets and parks tidy.

Letters, N Richards. I join with Alderman Leney in supporting the hopes of the Lord Mayor-designate, Ald Leo Port, that Sydney can be cured of its disease of littering.

The metropolitan area of Sydney must qualify for the dubious honour of being one of the world's most untidy cities. Not only litter, but daubed slogans and graffiti abound, e.g. the new railroad underpass at St Leonards has the walls defaced in this manner, and other examples could be cited ad nauseum.

Street and highway verges are made unsightly with litter, and, as far as a significant majority of the population is concerned, any beautification scheme means that the plants are ripe for stealing. Again quoting a St Leonards experience, within three days of a new garden being planted near the railway, several shrubs had been stolen.

The basic honesty of the people of Britain enables hanging flower baskets, street plantings, deck chairs at the seaside, etc, to remain for all to enjoy. In Europe it is the same, and one can travel hundreds of miles without seeing a piece of litter or dumped rubbish.

I have just returned home to Sydney badly disillusioned with my fellow citizens. Whatever laws we have for dealing with the problem are obviously lacking teeth.

Letters, Cecil Moyles. I would walk yards to put rubbish in a bin at the beach if there was a bin anywhere nearby. And if there is one such, then it is always overflowing. Can not municipal authorities see that people come to the beach at weekends, and need the bins emptied to stop this problem.

In the country, you can drive from Sydney to Newcastle, and not see a single bin. What should we do? Wait till we get to Newcastle, and then try to stuff our rubbish into the already full bins there.

Australians are no different from people anywhere. We all prefer tidy places, and will co-operate with anybody that encourages us. But we cannot put our rubbish into the bins if there **are** no bins.

Letters, Faye Frame. I agree with Cecil Moyles that we need more bins for rubbish. But the bins themselves are expensive, their servicing is expensive, and their maintenance is expensive. If we had ten times the population. Or if we had ten times the population density. Then we could afford a satisfactory number of bins.

But until then, we must realise that as an undeveloped country, some of the benefits of high populations are not available as yet.

THE RIGHT TO STRIKE

Letters, L Coster. The right to strike is well recognised and protected by law. **The right not to strike**, although equally protected by law, is not as well known. Many workers, beset by debts and knowing that it is not easy to find another job, would disobey strike calls if it was well publicised that they had every right to do so.

No worker is obliged by any law of the land to obey a strike call.

If governments and industry would emphasise and advertise this simple fact, it would encourage all those sensible men and women in certain strike-prone industries to defy the call.

Like other Western societies, we are too close to the precipice to go on tolerating the daily list of strikes. Before we start looking for extreme solutions, we should try the moderate strategy of persuading people to defy the madmen, and advising them that they have every right to do so.

OUR DICKENSIAN RAILWAYS

Railways keep popping up for criticism.

Letters, T Tatton. As a regular interstate rail traveller - I have travelled twice a year between Melbourne and Brisbane with large groups for the past 10 years - I had imagined myself well used to the deficiencies, as well as the undoubted pleasures, of this mode of travel.

One learns to accept the fact that major Expresses are almost invariably late on arrival, despite the absence of those variations in track, traffic, and weather conditions which affect road and air transport.

One learns to avoid the rudeness and inefficiency of staff and the 40-minute delays in the pig-trough buffet cars by taking packed snacks.

One even learns to endure the sea of garbage in the seating cars when the one small bin provided for a car seating 60 invariably overflows within the first two hours, and the lavatory floors awash in filth and uncleaned throughout the journey.

However, the last straw for me came on a recent Sunday when my party arrived at [Sydney] Central aboard the Brisbane Limited - late as usual - to transfer to the daylight Express for

Melbourne waiting across the platform. Amid the rush of transferring luggage for 50 people, loudspeakers told us we had one minute before departure. Requests to the nearest official for a delay were ignored.

As the train moved off, the last member of my party jumped on board, leaving on the platform a pile of luggage which happened to include the day's food and medicine for my infant son. The hostess on board possessed no such rarity as a baby's bottle, therefore my wife, carrying the baby, had to disembark at Strathfield. There, the station staff, leaving her to carry her burdens as best she could, and directing her to a platform from which no trains ran on Sunday, promised to phone Central about her luggage.

On arriving at Central, however, no one knew anything about the matter. She was directed first to the lost property section (closed on Sundays) then to the cloakroom (not concerned with luggage) and finally to the luggage room, where some unknown private person, to whom we are much indebted, had kindly booked the items on to Melbourne. My wife was graciously offered a seat on the night train, but told she would have to take up the possibility of a sleeping berth with the conductor on the train. She was then left to her own devices for the day.

> By contrast, within one hour of telephoning an airline office, she had been first placed on immediate standby, then found a seat on the next plane, assisted with infant and luggage, placed in a taxi and taken to Mascot to board a plane ready for departure. More of the same consideration and efficiency at Melbourne, and she was safely home within three hours.
>
> Such appalling performances by the railways must sadly but surely negate their attempts to create a new image and stem the steady loss of custom to the airways. Can these Dickensian relics not, by some means, be jolted into the twentieth century?

Comment. This Letter is very similar to the ones written since I started writing these books years ago. Since 1939, the Railways of Australia, every State, have been given the thumbs down for any aspect of service that you can think of.

THE TEMPO IS INCREASING

At the middle of September, the political situation got more chaotic. Fraser changed his cautious attitude to a double dissolution, and he, and most of the Liberals, became emphatic that elections should be called **now**.

This, of course, was an election for both Houses. On the polls, it might seem that the Liberals would win easily.

But Whitlam started to develop a different dodge. The nation should **hold an election just for the Senate**. From his point of view, it was **that body that was causing trouble by blocking Supply.** Get rid of it. Get a new body that was not troublesome. Hold an election only for the Senate.

But, I hear you point out, surely Whitlam would lose in a battle for the Senate,

No, not so, argued Whitlam There was **a change to Legislation just then** that allowed Senators from Northern Territory and Canberra for the first time. Whitlam could hope that he would win those new seats, and thus get control of the Senate.

To sum up his position. If he just kept his Lower House majority **and** got a new Senate with a Labor majority, then he had it all. What more could he want?

So, his new objective was **to campaign for a Senate (only) election**. Not for both Houses.

By the end of the month, policies on both sides had firmed and the wishes of both Parties were clear. Both wanted an election. **Whitlam wanted only the Senate to be up for grabs, and Fraser wanted both Houses.**

WHO CAN DECIDE ON WHAT WILL HAPPEN?

In general, the power to decide on what was becoming a constitutional matter, was with Queen Elizabeth II. Her representative in Australia was the Governor General.

Sir John Kerr was a barrister by training, who had been appointed to the position by Whitlam himself. He had a distinguished prior career, and had been in the position for just on a year.

He liked the pomp and ceremony of the office, and he wanted very much to be involved as far as possible in the politics of the day. He was inclined to drink more than his office suggested, and was deeply concerned in keeping his own tenure safe.

He was able to keep abreast of how the two Leaders were thinking with once-a-week formal meetings with each of them, but at more frequent social engagements that filled their calendars. Often these latter were not of a political nature, but were useful in providing information to him.

He was adept at consulting other legal experts, and had access to the finest brains in the nation. He had good relations with the office of the Queen, and used that to keep her informed of developments in Australia, and to **keep her informed of his opinion on them**.

To answer the question at the start of this section: Who can decide on what will happen, it was this gentleman, **the Governor General, Sir John Kerr, who will decide.**

OCTOBER NEWS ITEMS

Some parts of **Medibank** have been operating for three months. Other **parts are just starting on October 1st**. With that comes the threats of **strikes by honorary doctors** at major hospitals over contract issues....

The fights over the introduction are by no means over. **They could well worsen** as health-care workers realise just what changes will affect their purse strings and conditions.

The GIO, an Insurance giant in NSW, raised its fees for motor vehicle insurance across the board **by about 20 percent**. The previous increase had been **in January, when they increased by 30 per cent**....

Motorists should be pleased because it might appear that the rate of increase is getting less.

Unemployment increased to a new record for the third month in a row in September. **More nails for more coffins.**

Federal Ministers have received a notice from Parliament House officials to say that **their special cars are no longer available**. Previously, they had cars waiting for them when they finished the day....

Now they will be required to join a rank along with other non-Ministers....

Cost cutting even for the mighty.

Sydney City Council last night agreed to a proposal to study the creation of special areas inside its many parks for **the riding of skate boards**.... This would provide greater safety for both riders and pedestrians.

Five Sydney and Melbourne journalists have been missing for days at a small town, Balibo, in Portugese Timor.,,,

Now the bodies of four murdered men have been found. Due to the remoteness and poor communication, identification is difficult, but it is likely that **these are the missing journalists**....

Investigations are continuing.

Princess Margaret, as Chief Guide of the Girl Guides movement, was to parade before a mass of young girls in Canberra. She was early for the appointment and, not feeling well, stayed only for a while...

Unfortunately, **bus loads of Guides completely missed out** on their glimpse of her, and returned to the vast hinterland around Canberra disappointed.

The Irish Republican Army (IRA) is still creating trouble in Britain. As a reminder of this, consider that one of Britain's leading researchers into cancer was blown 15 yards and killed by a car bomb placed by the IRA. IRA damage caused in London was a constant menace to tourists and locals.

ABORIGINES AND THE POLICE

Earlier I mentioned that groups of lawyers were petitioning for a Royal Commission into the relationship between Police and Aborigines. The inference was that Police were to blame for bad situations.

Now we have a Letter that looks elsewhere for the reason.

Letters, S Shumack. In a four-page letter to the Federal Minister for Aboriginal Affairs, 18 Sydney lawyers have expressed grave concern for the Aboriginal-police relationship and are demanding a Royal Commission.

As one of three brothers who jointly served 103 years in the police force of this State, I gained a vast knowledge of the Aboriginal and his problems during my 39 years service. I say categorically that I have never known an Aboriginal offender to receive that treatment at variance with that of his white counterpart.

On the outskirts of a large country town of which I was the officer-in-charge was an Aboriginal settlement, the population of which was frequently augmented by an influx of Aboriginal seasonable workers. Apart from the usual troubles associated with drink and renegade whites, our relationship with these people was most cordial. I liked their sense of humour and their love of music, and many were my friends.

I have always entertained a great respect for the Aboriginal people and I urge the Government to give them a better deal. However, a Royal Commission is not the answer to their problems, for no Aboriginal pocket can ever hope to be "lined" by such an exercise. On the contrary, such inquiries are veritable bonanzas for the legal profession.

Like the 18 Sydney lawyers I, too, am concerned - not only for the plight of the original inhabitants of this country, **whose land was stolen from them by their white brothers**, but also for those unfortunate people who lost their life savings in trust funds. I would enjoin the 18 legal gentlemen to set about putting their own house in order, instead of bolsterng allegations of worsening Aboriginal-police relationship by snide innuendo; trust funds might then become what the name implies.

Letters, R Gibbes (former chaplain, Umbakumba, Northern Territory). May I warmly applaud Archbishop Loane's support of the call for a Royal Commission on Aborigines which was made by the Federal Minister for Aboriginal Affairs, Mr Johnson.

Especially did I join with the archbishop in asking for the terms of an inquiry to be broadened, and not limited to relations between Aborigines and the police.

I lived in an Aboriginal settlement, Umbakumba, at Groote Eylandt in the Gulf of Carpentaria, for four years until March this year. Having observed the scenes of riotous disorder there from time to time, I am sure nothing but good can come from a frank unveiling of the truth by a Royal Commission.

Recently I predicted that unless the drinking of liquor could be controlled at Umbakumba, then, despite the best intentions of the Government, backed by the pouring of large amounts of Government and trust funds into housing and other projects, the settlement was doomed. It would gradually disintegrate amid scenes of miserable degradation and squalor.

May the truth of all aspects of the Aboriginal situation be thoroughly uncovered, and may this be done with expedition. The Aborigines deserve our best.

Comment. But the more general view (rightly or wrongly) is that it is the Aborigines who were the problem.

COLLECT SUNSHINE IN A BOTTLE

It is well known that sunshine is good for you. If you get enough, then you benefit. If you do not, then perhaps you should try daylight saving. That is one of the arguments put forward in favour of this arrangement.

But the argument over this issue has waged every year since before WWII. At various times, some States have been in favour, and others against. Then in a few years, some have changed their mind. At no stage has there been a plan to have a uniform decision across the nation.

Thc NSW Premier has now gratuitously suggested that he might hold a referendum across the State on the matter.

This has opened up all the old arguments pro and con.

Comment. I forget whether he did have his referendum or not, but I can recall that in the next 50 years, the curtains certainly did fade.

SMOKING IN NON-SMOKING CARS ON TRAINS

Letters, P Brady. Polluting the atmosphere in trains and offending other passengers is not a god-given right. Let's crowd all smokers together rather than giving each the luxury of a comparatively clean atmosphere among two, three or whatever non-smokers..

If every smoker had to put up with everyone around him smoking and coughing, he would appreciate more the discomfort.

Further, I believe that there is a much greater incidence of coughing in smoking cars. I would like to hear a doctor's opinion if there is a greater chance of acting a cold, or other infection, by travelling in a car in which smoking is not prohibited.

Comment. You can see that there is only a small sign that smoking is a social menace.

And little sign that it is a health hazard.

In the world of 2025, smokers in offices, say, have to go outside and skulk in the alley if they want a puff. And anyone who lit up now in a train carriage would be set upon by all and sundry as soon as they started.

CROOKS ON COUNCILS

Letters, B Black. It seems to me that there are a lot of crooks on Local Councils. Am I right?

Comment. Some people say that things **never** change.

Supporters of this theory can draw comfort from the above Letter, where this opinion would find as much support, 50 years after the words were written, as they did at the time.

CONNOR IN STRIFE

Senator Rex Connor had been relatively quiet for a few months. As Minister for Minerals and Energy, he still had grand plans to develop our natural resources from the present back-yard operations into the huge industry that it has become since.

He had been frustrated because of lack of money through Treasury, and had dabbled with overseas money brokers. Chief among these was a gentleman called Kemlani, whose reputation was as yet unproven in Australia. Other Ministers, similarly frustrated, followed along the same path of enquiry with different brokers, though with no successes to date.

On May 20, in a meeting of the Government Executive Committee, **Connor had been instructed that discussions with Kemlani should cease**.

As far as Whitlam and the Government were concerned, the loan was off. And forgotten.

But not so for Kemlani, who received no official notice on the matter.

There things stood until October 10, when Kemlani gave a Press interview that indicated that **he and Connor were still in communication about the possibility**. Denials and accusations were issued from all parties, but the outcome was that at the end of October, Connor was summoned to Whitlam's office and dismissed.

The electorate was dumbfounded by this. Connor was very active and had a strong following. He had been apparently loyal to Whitlam when a few others were lukewarm about his leadership, and now he was gone.

Labor and the Press loved this. **They raised questions about the competence of the Government.** How could it happen that a Minister had been told to desist in a suspect activity, but had persisted? How could it happen that he had persisted for months, and had not told the Prime Minister? Or that the Prime Minister had not had notice of it from elsewhere? The questions went on and on.

As they persisted, they blew Fraser off the fence. He had been wavering about whether he should call for a double dissolution as soon as possible. This involved that he approach the GG and put his case. In this instance, it would be that the nation's economy was in a terrible condition with high unemployment, huge interest rates, strikes galore, and a frustrated population. On top of that, two Ministers had recently gone, and **the Kemlani affair showed that the Government simply could not manage**.

After such an accusation, the GG would need to ponder, perhaps negotiate with the leaders of the Parties, and then decide.

Given that prospect, Fraser decided to proceed, and in October he announced that a double dissolution would be the Liberal policy in future.

Needless to say, all prospects of a loan via Kemlani or any other broker was now off the table. Connor remained a back-bencher until next year, when he resigned his seat. He will be remembered for the grand idea that Australia could be a giant in the resources and energy sectors, much to the lasting benefit of the nation.

FRASER ACTS

The Government introduced a Bill to the Parliament that asked for the money to run the nation. That is, to guarantee Supply. It passed the House without trouble. But again it failed the Senate. And, said Fraser, the Liberals will block it next time as well. That would mean that Whitlam could go to the GG and ask for the dissolution of some part of the Parliament.

All Hell broke loose. Everyone in the nation had an opinion. And many of them voiced it. The newspapers and radio and TV were full of their thoughts and worries about the prospects. Some argued that there was not sufficient evidence of problems to justify such moves. Others argued that the GG had no power to intervene at all. Some said that it was not legal to grant a dissolution of a single House. Others argued that a Government that had been elected for three years should be allowed to run for three years.

A lot of these opinions were quite sensible. A lot were not. I enclose a few below of the sensible variety that were as typical as can be given the huge range of views.

Letters, D Altman, Sydney University. If Professor Lane's argument was taken seriously, it would justify the Senate forcing an election every time a government seemed unpopular - which would effectively ensure that no government would ever carry out the policies on which it was elected.

His letter fails completely to provide any justification as to why, for the first time in our history, there should be a premature election brought on against the desires of the Party which controls the House of Representatives. **It is control of that House which determines who governs**, and even Mr Fraser has felt constrained to produce better arguments than Professor Lane's misplaced populism to overrule this.

It is perhaps not surprising that Australian conservatives feel freer to tear up constitutional practice than do so-called radicals, the latest in this tradition being the Governor of Queensland who is now echoing the partisan rhetoric of his Premier. It is surprising that professors of constitutional law use their position to legitimise this.

Letters, R Jones. The Senate, as a responsible House of Parliament has not only a right, but a duty, to use any power which it lawfully has to remove that Government.

Letters (Mrs) L Johns. I'm taking the liberty of writing to defend the Government and Mr Whitlam. First, they won the election in what could be termed as a landslide, which at the time revealed the Australian voters' feelings regarding the former Government's management of the country.

What I want to point out is that they proceeded to do all in their power to rectify things and improve the conditions of the Australian people. In my view they succeeded to a large degree.

But recently the tide has turned throughout the Western world and Australia is no exception and has suffered its share of trouble. But **why blame the Government for inflation when it is world-wide,** and certainly much worse in Britain and America than it is here.

I read in the Press a few weeks ago that unemployment is at its worst level since the Great Depression, but what they failed to mention was the fact that the population was a third of what it is today.

I don't know Mr Whitlam personally but I feel I must defend him. He impresses as sincere and just in his words and actions.

Letters, D Perkins. We have seen in the last few months a concerted attempt by the Opposition political parties to ignite the passions of the Australian people. We are told repeatedly that the Government is virtually incompetent and that through some extraordinary circumstance it has relinquished its right to govern.

I cannot agree with this view.

In the few years since the Labor Party came to power, all has not been placid in public life. There have been mistakes and substantial errors in judgment; yet the Liberal-Country Party Coalition has also made the most gross and reprehensible errors in government.

It is in this sphere at present that the Opposition parties, full of indecent haste to regain the

Government benches, press disrespectfully ahead. It is a fearful sight to see such stolid parties sacrifice constitutional convention and propriety on the altar of expediency.

Letters, I MacFarlane. For two years, interrupted only by a double dissolution, the Government enjoyed the support of the people and **ran this country in such an inept manner** that it finally appears to have lost the support of the majority of electors.

During the last few months, when the Government realised that there is a very real chance of the Budget being blocked by the Senate, the Government has made its only responsible approach to governing this country.

If it is necessary for a convention to be disregarded to convince a government, any government, that the people of this country want good government all the time, then it is time that such conventions are broken.

To suggest that the breaking of this convention would lead to a breakdown of our democratic system or could lead to holding Federal elections every six months are the most reprehensible statements to come out of all the discussion by your many correspondents, and various politicians, on this issue. A willingness to reject Supply is a guarantee of responsible government.

No government which has governed wisely and well need ever fear the judgment of the people at the ballot box.

No opposition which does not consider that the government has lost the support of the people, and thereby its mandate to govern, would ever dare to block Supply and face the people at the ballot box.

Comment. No matter what the masses might think, it became obvious, as the month moved towards its end, that Fraser had decided to press for a double dissolution, and that Whitlam would be happy with a Senate only election.

All of this was gradually becoming apparent to the GG. He could see that he might be forced into making a decision soon. But, from his position, he was up against the clock, because the Budget had not been consummated. The Constitution said that it must be approved by mid-November, or else the whole nation would default on all its payments, and that would cripple it.

So, the GG was facing the situation where he had only three weeks to get the matter resolved. Time was running out.

NOVEMBER NEWS ITEMS

A large area of NSW and Victoria is under threat from **a hatching of locusts** due in the next few days. This will cause major devastation as the plague moves east eating everything in its path.

The **daughter of Japan's Emperor Hirohito** is now resident in Australia for the next three years. She is posted here by a major finance organisation. She is no longer considered royalty **because she married a commoner**.

In 1963, the discovery of bodies of two CSIRO employees were found after a New Years Eve party in Sydney's Lane Cove River raised a sensation. The cause has never been found. Yesterday, a serious claim was made that the eating of a puffer fish could be the cause....

Today, responsible authorities stated that puffer fish were definitely not involved....

The search goes on for the Bogle and Chandler murderers.

The Beatle Paul McCartney flew into Sydney. He was greeted by a crowd of about 15 persons. This is a lot different from the last time he arrived here 10 years ago. On that day, the huge crowd was hysterical.

The Queensland Premier is in Alice Springs for a visit. Last night he attended a function in his honour. While he was dining, about 100 Aborigines outside **"sang him to death"**, with an Aboriginal chant....

"**He should start dying from now on.** He will start dying now in body, mind and spirit. He is a finished man from now on. What he has done to blacks in Queensland is terrible."

The Department of Labour announced **statistics** that estimated that the unemployed in Australia would increase from the previous guess of 400,000, **up to the present guess of 600,000**....

With talk and thoughts of an election in all minds, **this was a disaster for Labor**.

NSW will be the second State (after Western Australia) to require that **chiropractors be licenced** by State authorities. The aim is to protect the public from **a growing number of quacks** who are not properly trained or qualified.....

It is thought that other dubious so-called professionals will soon be sorted out by similar legislation.

The Flying Doctor Service currently operates 22 aircraft, and flies 90,000 patients per year. About 40 per cent of these are Aborigines. It is having a difficult year financially, so if you see a request for funding, I urge you to give generously.

THE NEXT MONTH OF CHAOS

By the start of November, the entire nation was in a haze of maximum uncertainty. The previous fortnight had been beset with political manoeuvering, and posturing, and bluffing, and sometimes quiet bargaining. Phones ran hot, meetings were held, Press leakages were rampant, denials of impropriety were daily, and protestations of purity of motives were everywhere.

But still, at the start of November, a few things had been cleared up. Fraser, and his Liberals, were intending to block Supply. Fraser definitely wanted the dissolution of both Houses of Parliament, because he was confident that he could win both Houses. Whitlam wanted just a Senate vote, because he already held the House and thought that he might win the Senate.

The Governor General was waiting for some type of agreement between the Parties, and hoped that a breakthrough would happen **before** we had a real constitutional crisis. And, watching the clock, **before** the supply of money ran out on an effective date of mid-November.

LETTERS TO THE EDITOR

Every newspaper in this land was deluged with Letters. Most of them were highly emotional. Most of them were clearly partisan, with Labor voters supporting Whitlam, and Liberals supporting Fraser. Quite a few delved into British History to make some claim about precedents that had then been set, sometimes centuries ago. Others looked to supposed precedents that had been set by Australian History to date. Even including State Histories.

As an example, I have selected just two of the more rational Letters, that give an idea of what the sane respondents were thinking about. They do not in any way cover the full range of thoughts. That would take a book.

Letters, P Davis. Public opinion polls appear to show that voters in the nation's capital cities **have swung solidly back towards Labor**.

Yet absolutely nothing has changed in the state of the economy or in national morale during the past two months. We still have an alarming rate of unemployment, extremely dismal prospects for the new year, abnormally high inflation and the same Government which naively thought that borrowing an unprecedented mount of money from Arab nations would somehow overthrow the multi-nationals.

What then has changed to lure voters back to Labor?

In my view, it is the incredible efficiency of **the Government's new high-powered publicity machine**. This is where Mr Whitlam has done the Opposition "like a dinner." In the propaganda department, the Government has shown exceptional professionalism and dedication.

Just look at the record. **Aided by 303 highly-paid media professionals** (engaged as public servants to "explain" ministerial policies), the Prime Minister has very successfully diverted public attention from an appalling record, focused it on what he calls a constitutional crisis and convinced a large number of voters that:

* He is suddenly the Good Guy, defending the nation from a man set upon forcing a general election.

* Withholding Supply is illegal. It seems to matter little that Mr Whitlam sought to do exactly the same thing to bring down the Gorton Government. He failed because he could not rally enough support from the DLP, but his intention was clearly stated by him at the time.

* After three years in office, he is still entitled to a "fair go", despite an incredible succession of mistaken policies, ministerial blunders, reversed decisions and incompetence.

The propaganda machine has been equally successful in convincing people that the present Opposition has no right to "defy" convention. There is no mention of the ancient Westminster tradition that when a Government is caught in a major scandal (and few in this country or in Britain have equalled the loans affair), the Government resigns and submits to the judgment of the people.

Perhaps the biggest flaw in the campaign to make Mr Whitlam a "Good Guy" is his role in the loans affair. He signed the original illegal executive minute, and has since "accepted" the resignation of the two ministers charged with raising the loan. He continues to claim publicly that no charge of improper conduct has been raised against him. By airing this deceit at every possible opportunity, Mr Whitlam has convinced many people that he must be innocent.

It is clear the nation faces yet another crisis. The issue is this: does an elected Government have the right to create and exploit - at taxpayers' expense - a vast publicity machine devoted to sustaining it in office?

In my view, it does not. World history is studded with men who have risen to power on a barrage of lies, half truths and distortion. Most have come to a sticky end. Many have taken their country with them.

Letters, K Millar. Your poll concerning the Senate and Supply confirms a strong feeling among many people that **Mr Fraser has no real option other than to back off gracefully.**

Such action is unlikely to go against him after a short lapse of time - and may even further enhance the strong image he had previously built up.

It is readily agreed that the present Government must be the worst in most present voters' memories and that many of its actions and appointments have sunk to new moral depths.

There is no question that Mr Fraser has legality on his side, but politics is the art of the possible, and without the necessary groundswell of public opinion, pursuance of his course could be quite counter-productive.

I think that Mr Fraser must reassess and concentrate on the following priorities:-

* To achieve a solid victory in next year's half-Senate election;

* **To attain office in 18 months' time** and give good and honest government on a long-term basis.

Continuing grave disquiet about the loans and other "scandals" is not enough. It looks as though many people will have to dig in and survive as best they can for 18 months more - at least a continuing Senate majority can continue to block outrageous legislation.

Comment. This tiny sample gives an idea of the diversity of conflicting ideas that had the population unsettled.

Maybe the next few weeks will bring some resolution.

IS DISSOLUTION POSSIBLE?

The second week in November saw a number of attempts to avoid disaster. An interesting one was the suggestion that the **Government borrow funds from the banks**, and continue in business until something broke. It was a daring plan, and a few of the big banks said they would be happy to be involved. But the enormity of the sums involved caused everyone to rethink it all, and the plans collapsed.

Other suggestions involved the Senate allowing Supply, provided Whitlam promised a double dissolution within six months. Fraser stymied this by saying that he wanted a win now, not at some time in the future.

Finally, on November 11, the two Leaders at last met, with the hope that a face-to-face meeting would resolve the deadlock. But it failed. Each of them came out still firmly locked into their own position and it appeared that nothing would make them move.

But that appearance was wrong. The GG made sure of that much sooner than anyone expected.

NOVEMBER 11, 1975. A DAY IN HISTORY

Armistice Day is a historic day in Australia. It marks the end of WWI, and is honoured nation-wide by a one minute's silence across the nation.

Here it was marked also by a cessation of one type of hostility. But that was replaced by another, just as savage.

Fraser and Whitlam met at 9am, and over breakfast came to the conclusion that they still did not agree. Whitlam then rang the GG and requested an interview at 1pm, telling the GG they he would ask for permission to call for **a Senate election**.

He attended the GG at that time, and was met with

"before we go any further, I have to tell you that I have decided to terminate your commission."

Immediately after that, Kerr called in Fraser, who was waiting in another room. He commissioned Fraser as the new Prime Minister.

Whitlam still had control of the House, and it passed a resolution supporting Whitlam and not supporting Fraser, but Kerr rejected this, saying that the deed had been done, and that Fraser was already PM.

The news of these happenings was passed to the world about 4.30pm.

Whitlam was gone. Fraser was the new PM. The Government in power was the Liberals.

REACTIONS TO THIS NEWS

The nation was stunned. It went off to work today and, by the time it came home, the Prime Minister had been sacked and a stranger was the new incumbent. Ministers had to move out, lots of public servants lost their jobs, major projects somewhere on the drawing board were cancelled, and no one had the faintest idea of where the nation was headed.

Labor could not believe it. Surely Whitlam would come up with some scheme to re-install himself. Get rid **of** the GG, call in the Queen, enlist the Army. Where was the High Court when you needed it? Frustration gave way to rage at being cheated, so they said. Then they said "maintain the rage" and used this as a slogan for months, and even years, thereafter.

The Liberals could hardly believe it either. What a masterpiece, out of the blue. How great to get rid of the bullying arrogant PM, and his team of cowboys. How great it is to get sane, coherent government that knew the difference between sensible rules and chaos.

The Governor General must have felt a huge relief. His very careful plan to keep his job had succeeded. If anything had gone wrong, if there had been any disruptive counter attack at some stage in the dismissal, he could have been in hot water. But everyone took the situation like a flock of sheep. Phew!

THE PRINCIPALS SAID

Gough Whitlam:

"Ladies and gentlemen. Well may we say 'God Save the Queen' because nothing will save the Governor-General."

"The proclamation which you have just heard read by the Governor-General's official secretary was countersigned 'Malcolm Fraser', who will undoubtedly go down in Australian history from Remembrance Day, 1975, as Kerr's cur."

"....Clearly, the great issue, almost the sole issue of this campaign, will be whether the Government, which the people elect in the House of Representatives, will be allowed to govern from now on. The whole of this system is under challenge, as we see."

"I'm the first Prime Minister to be sacked for 200 years, since George III sacked Lord North."

Malcolm Fraser:

"It will be my sole purpose as head of the caretaker Government to restore responsible management to the nation's affairs, and to ensure that Australia has the General Election to which it is constitutionally entitled, and which has so far been denied it.

"There will now be an election as the Constitution requires. The great defence of our democracy is that the Constitution must be upheld.

"The Australian people will have their say. The choice is theirs at the ballot box."

Sir John Kerr:

"The decisions I have made were made after I was satisfied that Mr Whitlam could not obtain Supply. No other decision open to me would enable the Australian people to decide for themselves what should be done."

".... the people can do what, in a democracy such as ours, is their responsibility and duty, and theirs alone. It is for the people to decide the issue which the two leaders have failed to settle."

A FEW QUESTIONS ON THE DISMISSAL

Comment. I will not enter into a discussion of who were the goodies and baddies. Hundreds of people have done this and still do. But I will add a few observations after studying hundreds of the writings.

Why did not Whitlam appeal to the Queen? Because he was a champion of the cause that Australia must stand on its own feet. To appeal to the Queen would acknowledge a subservience he did not accept.

Did the GG have the power to sack a duly elected Government? He did. That is one of the powers that come with the job.

Could and should the GG have done anything to avert this dismissal? It is often said that he neglected his duty **by not consulting with Whitlam in the lead up**. It was convention that the GG must do this on matters of importance. Yet the decision to sack him remained a closely guarded secret until the moment it was issued.

There was a host of other questions and arguments that were advanced. They make great reading, and I commend them to you.

LAST WORDS ON THE DISMISSAL

When the immediate dust had settled, there was a new government in this fair nation, with a new team of new leaders. We will have to wait to see how they turn out. **But before that, they have to get elected again, in a couple of weeks, before Christmas.** The politicians will not have much time to lick their wounds, or to exult, before they are faced with the results of the double dissolution. That is, a general election on December 14.

So, Labor should forget that dismissal. That's history. Get on with winning at the next poll. **But that was impossible for a voter who had been committed for at least two more years to a national hero.** It was still at the forefront of Labor's mind. Every time a person spoke of what might happen in the future, within a minute, discussion came back to the jumble of the dismissal. For example, Whitlam opened his campaign for re-election with the statement that the main issue would be the dismissal.

He wanted **all voters, be they Labor or Liberal**, to **forget their former allegiances to Parties**, but to vote instead on what he saw as the injustices of his dismissal.

Fraser, by contrast, sought to use the tried-and-true formula of entering peoples' lives through their hip pockets. He promised tax cuts in each of the next three years, and generous home savings grants. He made only passing references to the dismissal.

Meanwhile, the rest of the population sought to revert to normalcy. The Governor General received three different mail bombs, and he started his very long campaign **to publicly deny any guilt for the dismissal**.

The new Treasurer, Phillip Lynch, was greeted by the threat of strike action by 1,000 anxious Public Servants working in the Treasury. They were Laborites who resented the Liberal victory. A petition was started in Canberra demanding the GG resign.

And in New Zealand, a bad omen for Labor when the sitting New Zealand government was unseated in national elections, suffering a landslide loss of 21 seats.

Like I said, back to normal.

DECEMBER NEWS ITEMS

Norman Gunston, sometimes known as Garry McDonald, was awarded the Best Entertainer of the Year.

Two brothers, gold prospectors all their lives, found the **biggest nugget of pure gold this century**. It weighed 2,520 Ounces, and was about the size of a Queensland Blue pumpkin.

Nabiac is a small country town up the NSW coast that is famous for nothing. It does have a ladies tennis club, however. 16 members always dob in 50 cents a week to buy lottery tickets....

It paid off. **They won the first Opera House Lottery**, and will share $250,000 between them. Their plans include **a night out with their husbands**.

The Hordern Pavilion in Sydney saw a near-riot as thousands of mothers and their pre-teen children turned out to **see the Bay City Rollers perform**....

Apparently, *Bye Bye Baby* was a big hit.

Do you fancy a donkey for Christmas? The owner of the Dural Park (Sydney) Donkey Stud says that donkeys are docile, easy to handle, hardy, disease-free, requiring a minimum of upkeep....

This weekend, 140 of them will be for sale at Homebush Markets. Here is your chance....

But the Market owner says **these wild donkeys** from the Northern Territory might not be suitable for children....

So perhaps you might like to be a bit careful.

The referendum on daylight saving in NSW **will** go ahead. If successful, the saving will start in October.

The ABC has announced that **the Evening News will start at 6.40pm next week**. Not at 7pm....

This is to fit in with Test Cricket from Perth for the five days....

ABC TV producers will refuse to co-operate because they **do not think the cricket should be given priority over News**. Especially at the vital time of a general election.

A motorist, driving at night, **hit and killed a horse** being led along the road. It was on its way to Randwick racecourse for early-morning training....

The owner sued for damages. The motorist was **ordered to pay $70,000 (in 1975 currency)**. The horse, quite successful in racing, had the potential to earn large sums from standing at stud.

The Lock Ness monster has held the local population in fear for a century. There have been myriads of theories as to its existence and origin. A British researcher now claims that he has photos that confirm it is **the remains of a Viking boat**.

TOP MOVIES IN 1975

JAWS
Roy Sneider, Robert Shaw

ONE FLEW OVER THE CUCKOO'S NEST
Jack Nicholson, Louise Fletcher

NASHVILLE
Keith Carradine, Karen Black

MONTY PYTHON AND THE HOLY GRAIL
Graham Chapman, John Cleese

THE ROCKY HORROR SHOW
Tim Curry, Susan Sarandon

THREE DAYS OF THE CONDOR
Robert Redford, Faye Dunaway

FRENCH CONNECTION II
Gene Hackman, Fernando Rey

RETURN OF THE PINK PANTHER
Peter Sellers, Christopher Plummer

DOG DAY AFTERNOON
Al Pacino, Charles Cazale

BARRY LYNDON
Ryan O'Neal, Marissa Berenson

APPLE DUMPLING GANG
Bill Bixby, Susan Clark

THE MAN WHO WOULD BE KING
Sean Connory
Michael Caine

TOP SONGS IN 1975

"Mamma Mia"	ABBA
"January"	Pilot
"Fox on the Run"	Sweet
"Please Mr Postman"	The Carpenters
"My Little Angel"	William Shakespeare
"Summer Love"	Sherbet
"Love Will Keep Us Together"	Captain and Tenille
"The Newcastle Song"	Bob Hudson
"I Do, I Do, I Do, I Do, I Do"	ABBA
"Horror Movie"	Skyhooks
"Bye Bye Baby"	Bay City Rollers
"Before the Next Teardrop Falls"	Freddy Fender

HERE COME THE ELECTIONS

December is here and the election campaign is in full swing. Nothing really new is happening, but the air is full of excitement. That is because everyone - and I mean everyone - sees the election as the culmination of the goings on that have so absorbed the nation for half a year. It is like a script written slowly and deliberately, a real-life fictional story, that unfolded like a newspaper serial.

In retrospect, readers could see what was inevitable. There were swings and roundabouts all over the place, but the central theme was obvious. A wildly ambitious new government got giddy with power and tried to do too much. In doing this, they wrecked the economy of the nation and wreaked havoc. Soon enough, their opponents got their act together and used the holes, in **every** constitution, to get rid of the existing government.

And now, titillated readers, who also happen to be voters, are all agog to find out the final chapter. Will they collectively give their approval to that previous Opposition (the Liberals) and vote them in? Into both Houses?

Or will the previous incumbents (Labor) maintain the rage, and stay with the once godlike figures of two years ago?

Or will they vote for a bit of both worlds, and end up with a hung Parliament - again?

WHAT DO LETTER WRITERS THINK?

There were plenty of these. They were mainly statements of long-held biases, enraged or excited by recent events. I have omitted Letters that were just letting off steam, or hurling abuse.

Letters, (Mrs) B Oliver. Should the Labor Party not be re-elected, will they stand by their insistence that **an elected party should stay in office for three years**, or will they do their utmost, backed up by the unions, to remove it from Government?

Is there one rule for the Labor Party when in office and another when not?

Letters, R McDonald. I feel compelled to point out the economic absurdity of the present Liberal Party advertising campaign.

Following a period when prices have greatly increased, but average incomes increased in excess of prices, the last thing we need is for the public to be encouraged to feel that they are entitled to a larger income.

This is a classic example of the naivete of economic thinking that pervades so much of our community, particularly from a section of it that should know better.

It is not the actual cost of an item that counts, but the relationship it has to average incomes. To quote, in this respect "we have never had it so good".

Letters, (Mrs) R Farquhar. The generally accepted meaning of those emotive expressions "coup d'etat" and "putsch" (despite the learned lexicographers) is seizure of government of a State by force, almost always with Army support and customary display of hardware.

When, I wonder, did the tanks roll up to Government House or Parliament House and oust Mr Whitlam and his Ministers, and instal a new and permanent regime with unlimited powers, and why is there to be a free general election shortly to establish what sort of government the Australian people want here and now?

Mr Whitlam's facile toungue has run away with him again and I hear from a friend in Scotland that he has even invaded the airwaves **there**; every time she turns on her TV, there he is declaiming about coups and putsches and how he wuz robbed.

Letters, E Browne. It seems from your editorial of November 25 that the Herald's idea of democracy differs from what many of us have been led to believe. Heretical as it may be to disagree with *The Sydney Morning Herald*, but between mid-October and the 11th of November attacks were made on the notion of parliamentary representation of the people:

(1) By virtue of a majority that was neither elected nor representative, the Australian

people were denied the right of knowing how their elected representatives in the Senate would have voted on the money bills.

(2) A duly elected representative government was dismissed by a man (the GG) who is no way accountable to the people.

I am astonished that Australians, whatever their political colour, can regard these processes, however legal or constitutional in the narrow sense, as being democratic.

Letters, G McFarlane and 56 others, Wesley College. Mr Fraser has caused, and Sir John Kerr collaborated in, a serious attack on our democratic system; the people of Australia must assert their belief in our constitutional democracy if it is not to be slowly and surely destroyed in the coming years. We believe that Mr Whitlam should be re-elected with a majority in both Houses on these issues alone.

TRIUMPH FOR LIBS

The headline from Sunday's *Sunday Herald* bore the above headline.

Its by-line read

FRASER WINS IN A LANDSLIDE

The next day, the *Sun Herald* carried the detail that Fraser had a 53 seat majority in the House. It was too early yet to give figures for the Senate, but the Liberals had romped it in there as well.

In the House, the majority is the biggest in the nation's history. **In the Senate**, the Liberal majority is big enough for the Liberals to control it without any help .

In the Labor Party, six of its Ministers lost their seats. Whitlam will not resign, but is already vowing to win back control in three years' time. Fraser aims to have talks with Heads of Departments to start the changes in policies and personnel that will occur. Incumbent ministers will need to vacate their offices, and reams of letters with their letter-heads will be wasted.

But, it is all over. Labor is no longer in power.

Whitlam is no longer God, as he was two years ago. He is no longer god, as he was one year ago. He is just another ex-Prime Minister, and will be for three years to come.

CHRISTMAS SEEMS TO COME EVERY YEAR

The Chrismas shopping is just about done. Mum did not faint in the crowd, her family have said they will all arrive in time to eat, Dad has bought a lot of grog, the turkeys in the back yards are looking nervous, children are all salivating. Looks like a great Christmas. Noisy, but great.

This year I am looking at gifts for sophisticated mothers. Last year I bought a swag of loot for children, but that was a loud disaster. But not this year. It's all sophistication. I share my thoughts with you.

Repair Jewellery - It's Worthwhile!

The price of jewellery has risen so astronomically that it's well worthwhile having your old jewellery repaired - or remodelled. **Robin A Restorations** can remake any piece - yet, as they are manufacturing jewellers, they charge only wholesale prices, so it'll be within your budget allowance. Just look at that cluttered old brooch you inherited. You'll never wear it, yet it has several diamonds and can be turned into a glittering ring. Also, they can remodel wedding rings by retaining the old ring in the design - it's just made wider!

A Pregnant Pause!

Are you geared for Christmas Party time? We've noticed that there are some stunning long or medium length party dresses at **Lady Grayson's Maternity Boutique** - perfect whether you're expecting or not! There's a gorgeous long Pucci-style print in jersey at

$55.95, and a heavenly voile style in white with a scattered flower pattern, contrasted with borders of plain colour denim in blue or carrot. As well, we liked a short dress in calico with lace insertions at $36.50 - and for the pool, swim-suits in one or two piece styles.

Look Great in Cotton or Jersey.

The most popular fashions for Summer are undoubtedly in cotton or jersey - so it's nice to know that you'll find stacks of them at **Molly Newman's.** Sketched is a graceful dress in Eau de Nil jersey, just one of the many superb dresses for the mother of the bride for morning, noon and evening weddings. As well, we noticed a charming Sea Island long style at $35.99, and unusual long skirts and tops, as well as super smart day length skirts, some in wrap-over styles. The second sketch features an attractive shirt dress at $79.99 - other fashions by **Carla Zampati,** imported Estacels and Lucas fashions at REDUCED prices; sizes of fashions, 8 to 28.

SUMMING UP 1975

So, 1975 has come and gone. What a pity it has gone, because I really enjoyed reporting it. It had so much happening, with a trick round every corner. My big regret is that there was so much to write about that I could not fit into this book. I could easily have written another book, about the last two months alone, if there had been space. Still, it was great while it lasted.

My most enjoyable part was the researching and writing about the three principal characters. If this book had been complete fiction, **I could not have invented three such attention-grabbing heroes.** Each of them was obsessed with winning, self-centred to a manic point. Each of them was fully determined that he was right, and at the same time, certain that **his** way was the right way for the nation as well. And then the trick ending, with the election being needed, and won, by a stop-the-rot do-nothing Party.

All of this was accomplished by a nation fully involved, with bitterness and violent arguments and long-lasting recriminations. Yet not a single shot was fired, street demonstrations resulted in only two cans of beer and a good spit hitting one leader, and a couple of Ministers who asked for it, being sacked.

All Australians should be proud of the way we handled 1975, a year of political crisis. It was a great demonstration of how democracy, at its best, works.

Let us all resolve to keep it working that way.

COMMENTS FROM SERIES READERS

Tom Lynch, Spears Point.....Some history writers make the mistake of trying to boost their authority by including graphs and charts all over the place. You on the other hand get a much better effect by saying things like "he made a pile". Or "every one worked hours longer that they should have, and felt like death warmed up at the end of the shift." I have seen other writers waste two pages of statistics painting the same picture as you did in a few words....

Barry Marr, Adelaide....you know that I am being facetious when I say that I wish the war had gone on for years longer so that you would have written more books about it...

Edna College, Auburn.... A few times I stopped and sobbed as you brought memories of the postman delivering letters, and the dread that ordinary people felt as he neared. How you captured those feelings yet kept your coverage from becoming maudlin or bogged down is a wonder to me....

Betty Kelly. Every time you seem to be getting serious you throw in a phrase or memory that lightens up the mood. In particular, in the war when you were describing the terrible carnage of Russian troops, you ended with a ten line description of how aggrieved you felt and ended it with "apart from that, things are pretty good here". For me, it turned the unbearable into the bearable, and I went from feeling morbid and angry back to a normal human being....

Alan Davey, Brisbane....I particularly liked the light-hearted way you described the scenes at the airports as the American high-flying entertainers flew in. I had always seen the crowd behaviour as disgraceful, but your light-hearted description of it made me realise it was in fact harmless and just good fun.

MORE INFORMATION ON THESE BOOKS

Over the past 17 years the author, Ron Williams, has written this series of books that present a social history of Australia in the post-war period. They cover the period for 1939 to 1975, with one book for each year. Thus there are 37 books.

To capture the material for each book, the author, Ron Williams, worked his way through the *Sydney Morning Herald* and *The Age/Argus* day-by-day, and picked out the best stories, ideas and trivia. He then wrote them up into 180 pages of a Year-book.

He writes in a direct conversational style, he has avoided statistics and charts, and has produced easily-read material that is entertaining, and instructive, and charming.

They are invaluable as gifts for birthdays, Christmas, and for the oldies who are hard to buy for.

These books are available at all good book stores and newsagents. They are listed also in all leading catalogues, including Title Page and Dymocks and Booktopia.

ALSO FROM THE AUTHOR at jen@bookbooks.biz

THERE ARE 37 TITLES IN THIS SERIES

For the 37 years from 1939 to 1975

Chrissie and birthday books for Mum and Dad, and Gran and Pop, and Aunt and Uncle, and cousins, and family and friends, and work, and everyone else.

Don't forget a good read and chuckle for yourself.

In 1945, the Japs gave up and the Germans gave up. In Oz, every Jap was hated for the next twentyyearsatleast.Bulldogging and buckjumping were quite popular, the distinction between Communism and Socialism was not all the clear. The Brits were starving, and our own Bundles for Britain helped a lot. Rubber tyres for cars and bikes will be on sale next year, rationing of silk stockings will be abolished. Could the world get any better?

In 1955, be careful of the demon drink, get your brand new Salk injections, submit your design

for the Sydney Opera house now, prime your gelignite for another Redex Trial, and stop your greyhounds killing cats. Princess Margaret shocked the Church, Huxley shocked the Bishops, and our Sundays are far from shocking.

In 1965. Winston Churchill died. Relatives from Gallipoli and Greece and Crete did not all mourn. Maybe we should cancel Anzac Day marches because of heavy drinking. Hemlines are going up, exposing "spiritual knees and legs". Dawn Fraser took the flag in Japan, and ball-point pens were not coming to a school near you. Alphabet soup was filling bowls, and school projects were irritating corporations.

In early 1975, Whitlam had led the Parliament for a year. His shine was starting to tarnish, and he was no longer seen as God, but as god. In the meantime, the economy was nearly ruined, half a million people were on the dole, and interest rates on home loans were 17 percent. His Ministers kept on making big changes, and some of them were sensible. Towards the end of the year, he had a long-running fight with Malcolm Fraser, and the Governor General. He lost both of these, and was pensioned off as Prime Minister.